MALTA
A panoramic history

A NARRATIVE HISTORY OF
THE MALTESE ISLANDS

By the same author:

Felix Culpa: a novel of contemporary Catholic life in the USA.
Exposition Press, Hicksville, New York, 1976.

Malta & Gozo Explained to Extraterrestrials and Other Aliens.
Media Centre, Malta, 1988.

Personality Development: a socio-psychological study of man.
Media Centre, Malta, 1990.

The Loggia of Malta: a historical novel set in 16th century Malta under
Grand Master Martino Garzes. Publishers Enterprises Group (PEG) Ltd,
Malta, 1992.

Jiena Nemmen fija Nnifsi: a book on positive thinking.
Colour Image Press, Mġarr, Malta, 1993.

Il-Bxara t-Tajba skond San Miżun: the Malta Dead Sea Scrolls.
Media Centre, Malta, 1993.

Joseph S. Abela

MALTA
A panoramic history

A NARRATIVE HISTORY OF
THE MALTESE ISLANDS

Publishers Enterprises Group (PEG) Ltd

Publishers Enterprises Group (PEG) Ltd
P.E.G. Building, UB7 Industrial Estate,
San Ġwann SGN 09

First edition 1997
Second edition 1999

ISBN: 99909-0-067-1

Phototypeset and printed in Malta by P.E.G. Ltd

Acknowledgements

The author gratefully acknowledges the cooperation of:

Charles Meilaq (Advantage Advertising)
Kevin Cauchi (DOI Office)
Rev. Karm Zammit (Vice-Rector, St Paul's Church, Valletta)
Stanley Spiteri (photographer)
Paul Mizzi (Klabb Kotba Maltin)
Rev. Joseph Saliba (Carmelites)
Rev. Vito Borgia (Greek Catholic Church, Valletta)

Contents

Introduction

History students are usually made to wade through volumes of dry facts and still drier dates and all they end up doing, over many years of study, is hate that subject called history. The many events they have to remember and the many dates they have to learn by heart and the many protagonists who did what to whom are enough to set a student off the love of a subject that should be enjoyable and enlightening.

Such history students turned history haters, however, will be relieved to know that there is another perspective from which history can be considered. This is the *panoramic* aspect, which is the one adopted in this particular book.

In this approach, rather than meticulous details as to dates and personages and who did what and when, we take a comprehensive, overall view of a period and analyse the most important contribution that that particular period of time made to the overall conduct of the nation. This is done in view of the fact that it is the accumulation of such layers of history that go to make up that nation's *collective psyche*.

In the case of Malta, we hope that this version will meet a very much-felt need for there has never been a similar study to date of our history for the English reading public.

As luck would have it, Malta's history can easily be divided into such segments because historically they are all plainly clear-cut.

Thus we start with Pre-history and for this we have the various temples whose builders have left us their testimony in stone to guide us. Then we proceed into the historical array of nations that held sway over Malta: the Phoenicians, Romans, Byzantines, Arabs, Normans, Anjevins, Aragonese, Hospitallers, French and finally the British. After all, these many nations that ruled over Malta have left their mark on these islands. Finally we come to the modern, independence and post-independence eras and see how these are affecting the modern Maltese.

So in a way the various historical landmarks are there in plain view, to be duly explained. And yet, barring some very special and key events, we avoid burdening the reader with dates, for such is not the purpose of this book. We want to familiarize those, especially among the foreign readers who are interested in the various influences that the various foreign powers who ruled over Malta left behind them, how all this has gone into forming part of the patrimony of this nation as part of its collective psyche. And hence how all this goes to explain, partly at least, why the Maltese today act and behave and believe the way they do.

We will stick to the overall essentials without getting bogged down in details, and this is done in a style that, it is hoped, is far removed from pedantic pomposity or fake scholarliness but moves along with a facile pen.

It is hoped, indeed, that this will make the reading of history enjoyable: a task that if our school-days are to serve as an indication, is not too often the case in any student's life. Rather, it has pushed us to hate that subject called history; which is a thousand pities. For history is life, history is living. History is one of the most important and interesting and fascinating subjects that one can dig one's teeth into.

And talking about school-days. On a personal note, I must say that I feel very lucky to have had back then at the Lyceum as mentors two of Malta's foremost historians to instill this love of history in me: Salvino Laspina and Andrew Vella. The former with this definitive text-book *Outlines of Maltese History* provided many a student with a first introduction to Malta's varied and exciting past, while the latter with his *Storja ta' Malta*, published an authoritative history of Malta in Maltese.

To round off the picture I must also acknowledge my debt of gratitude to Mr. Joseph S. Ellul for allowing me to literally pick his brain and his book *Malta's Pre-diluvian Culture* with permission to reproduce the theories and diagrams in Chapter 1. History teacher Mr. Vincent Zammit who patiently went over the manuscript with a fine tooth-comb to point out all the inaccuracies and Anthony R. Callus for his invaluable help in checking for other kinds of mistakes deserve my thanks as well. Now I have no one to blame but myself for the ones that got through.

Joseph S. Abela,
Valletta.

October, 1995.

Fourth Centenary Year of the Building of the
Jesuit **Collegium Melitense** at Valletta,
otherwise known as **the Lyceum.**

Fourth Centenary Year of the death of
Grand Master Jean Parisot de la Vallette,
one of the most illustrious that ruled the Order.

Chapter 1

The Age of Megabuilders

(Pre-historic caves and temples – before time began)

In the beginning.... In a way, the title of this section, *pre-historic*, is a contradiction in terms: how can anything be said or written about a place or people before history actually begins to unroll? We know of course that what is normally meant by pre-history is that period of time when there are no written documents to go by and very few other indicators to show us what life was really all about. In fact information is so sparse and the grounds for the conclusions arrived at are so slender that various and sometimes opposing theories can he held about that particular period – which plunges us straight into controversial polemics.

For the pre-historic era is tricky in the sense that evidence can be interpreted to prove or disprove even at times a stand hitherto accepted as viable theory.

So for the interpretation of this particular *pre-historic* era of Malta we need the help of archaeologists more than anybody else for we are not dealing with written *historical* documents but with stone constructions. These very stones, however, in themselves and under the scrutiny of the experts, can yield precious information that can equal that of historical documents.

Luckily for Malta, its unwritten history is documented in its magnificent temples – some of which are among the best examples

of primitive man's handiwork and also among the oldest free-
standing temples in the world: a truly inestimable and priceless
patrimony not only for Malta but for all mankind. All to be found in
tiny Malta, and still tinier Gozo.

So it is from the study of these temples that we can come to
some conclusions about early life in Malta: their possible purpose;
their mode of construction; their particular alignment to which
heavenly bodies (lunar/solar); their particular location and such
details. Archaeologists continuously study all these factors to draw
sometimes tentative, sometimes pretty certain conclusions about
such pre-historic periods – conclusions, it bears repeating, that
do not always bear the mark of complete certainty, because the data
to be interpreted can be so mysterious and elusive at the same
time.

The traditional three-fold division

There are some scholars who tentatively yet neatly classify Malta's
pre-history into a three-fold division – according to the different
periods in which various tools were found that must have been used
for the construction and/or refurbishment of the temples and
surrounding habitations. This must necessarily remain tentative and
subject to periodic scholarly revision as more finds come to light or
as more theories gain acceptance. According to the different periods,
then, would be placed the various localities where temples were built
or archaeological finds were made. The three-fold division is into
the general ages known as: Neolithic (Stone), Chalcolithic (Copper)
and Bronze.

This very schematic proposal runs right away into trouble with
some specialists who assert, for example, that a site in which certain
copper instruments were found, does not exclude the fact that this
same site might have been inhabited earlier by Stone Age people,
only to be kept on as a habitation/temple site in later eras. One has
to make allowance for the fact that on the same site, various layers

in various stratigraphic periods have succeeded each other. So, such a schematic and neat division does not always find too much backing today.

Towards a new perspective

If one takes an archaeological/geological site like Għar Dalam, for example, one finds that it has yielded archaeological data in the shape of fossils that go back to hundreds of thousands of years that cannot be pigeon-holed into any of the three categories above. In fact, scholars aver that Għar Dalam is a special case in and of itself, and a source of inestimable archaeological material that is helping us revise the historical origins of the Maltese Islands.

First of all, that Għar Dalam as a cave must have been in existence hundreds of thousands of years ago is beyond doubt; if nothing else from the well-preserved and bountiful stalagmites and stalagtites to be found at the site. Now the rate at which these form is well-known and this can confirm the conclusion of the eons it must have taken to come to their present size. But at Għar Dalam there are also indications of other material that does not date back to the origins of the stalagmites and stalagtites but came in later, successive ages.

Hence, the first obvious conclusion: at Għar Dalam, there are different layers which denote different time-periods, sometimes eons apart, in this same locality. To take an example: there is a mass of stalagmitic matter about a foot high but there is also a much larger base where various (animal) bone-layers have been unearthed and then other layers which definitely point to human habitation. All this shows that between the settling of these several layers, from stalagmatic mass to human habitation, several hundreds of thousands of years must have passed. The evidence pointing to the presence of man at this cave also points to the theory that he must have been the more recent resident for we know that primitive man must have first lived in caves, not in man-made constructions. And

Għar Dalam was just one such primitive natural site in Malta giving shelter to a primitive species of man.

There are indications, such as the finds discovered on the surface area in this cave that belong to a later period, that testify to this. The deeper and much older layers at Għar Dalam which consist of alluvial deposits, must have been formed earlier: probably made by a free-flowing river that at times meandered underground through this area.

This neatly explains the presence of skeletons and fossils of huge animals at this deeper layer, animals and skeletons that must have been carried by the river currents.

However, even this neat explanation comes across two formidable difficulties: how could the limited territory available here have accommodated animals that were far too large (like hippos, pygmy elephants) to have inhabited such small islands as Malta and Gozo? Besides, such huge animals needed vast tracts of pasture-land and territorial nesting-grounds. Again how could such skeletons be carried by rivers? If the Maltese Islands blatantly lack anything, it is rivers. For a very simple reason: there are no mountains in the territory. So how could a river be meandering underground forcefully dragging these skeletons to be fossilized in this particular cave?

The answer to these queries lies in putting some geological factors together which point unfailingly in the direction that the Maltese Islands must have been joined to the land mass to the North as well as to the land-mass to the South: Malta, Gozo, Comino and Filfla (as well as Sicily, Pantelleria and all the other big and small islands) were once part of a land-bridge or rather a land-mass – as was the whole of what is today known as the Mediterranean Sea. And this explains the presence in the Maltese Islands of fossils of animals that date back to hundreds of thousands of years: these animals must have roamed freely across this land-mass and they could migrate as climate and weather dictated.

And yet, if there was one whole land mass linking the Maltese Islands perhaps both to North Africa and the rest of Europe, what happened to turn this land-mass into islands surrounded by a sea?

The Great Flood theory

Certain archaeologists/historians theorize that the biblical flood besides being a cataclysmic down-pour of long duration was also a true and real flooding in the truest sense of the word: namely that that bit of land once joining present-day Gibraltar with North Africa, at the points known as 'the Pillars of Hercules' even to the Ancients, caved in. As a result the Atlantic Ocean flooded into the Mediterranean cascading in gigantic waterfalls and torrential inundations as the deluge forcefully carried everything in its wake.

The force of this wave as it rippled eastwards through the Mediterranean area sank whole tracts of land along with many settlements, animal and human, as it rushed along. The pre-existing few lakes in the Mediterranean basin were flooded so that now they were joined into one big lake i.e. the Mediterranean Sea. The existing smaller lakes, like the Caspian Sea became bigger because they were flooded and their level rose higher while the high plateaus or mountain-tops jutting up to heaven became the islands that dot the Mediterranean basin. The deep canyon-valleys of the land mass were filled in with water that became the deeper tracts of the Mediterranean Sea. (This perhaps could have given risen to the many legends about the buried cities like Atlantis, although such legends could equally be the result of any of the periodic earth movements due to gigantic volcanic upheavals and tremors, that shake the Mediterranean basin from time to time).

Confirmation of the theory of the inundations from the flood comes from an unexpected quarter for it is modern oil-drilling that adds credence to this theory. Geologists drilling for oil bore the sea-bed for geological floor samples as a matter of course at different levels before actually undertaking the expensive task of large-scale

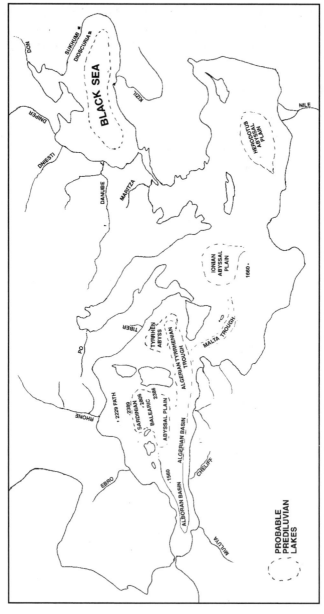

Sketch map of the Pre-diluvian mediterranean showing probable fresh water lakes and the Rift Valley at the Gibraltar Gate drilling. While drilling off the Mediterranean Basin near Spain, geologists discovered in some such samples recovered from the sea-bed the fossilized remains of some type of amoebic creature that has to date been found only on the surface areas of the desert in Death Valley (California, U.S.A.), for this particular creature survives only on the desert floor. Hence, these geologists concluded that the sea-bed – at least off Mediterranean Spain – at one time must have been exposed to the vicissitudes and conditions of life on land (and very probably desert conditions as well), for this fossilized creature is not native to the sea-bottom.

A feather in the cap of those who hold that there was a time when sections of the surface-area of what is today the Mediterranean Sea was not covered by water. Or conversely that there were areas that must have been once solid ground: plateaus or deep valleys.

So it is not unthinkable that the islands of Malta and Gozo (and Pantelleria and Sicily and Sardinia and Corsica and Mallorca and Minorca) at one time were part of a continuous land mass that linked modern-day Europe to modern-day Africa and that Għar Dalam was the inner recess of a river that flowed from the mountains surrounding and linking Malta. Hence the fossilized skeletons that drifted with the river flow and that must have passed through Għar Dalam and that got embedded in the river-bottom there: buried forever, or till archaeologists unearthed them.

(By sheer good luck, the author has a copy of a Nazi War Archives film that shows that at one time Germany discussed the possibility of reversing the Flood Theory process: by damming the Mediterranean Sea at the Dardanelles, Suez and Gibraltar by means of gigantic turbines, the Nazis planned to pump the sea-water into the desert, thus creating enough dry land so that the German Army could march across, on land, from Germany to North Africa. It was only the practical consideration that the enemy could blast the dams and destroy the best laid plans that deterred them from realising this course of action.)

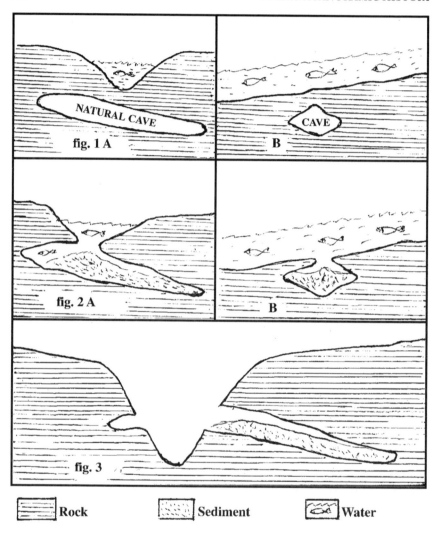

Rock   Sediment   Water

The probable progressive formation of Għar Dalam in three periodic stages

So much for the deeper layers at Għar Dalam. As to the presence of the other geological layers, the explanation is at hand as well. This naturally protected site could have served for many centuries as a shelter for the animals that roamed freely between Europe to the North and Africa to the South – because these two geographical areas, it seems, were all connected together by land and were one land mass. Especially since the remains – both fossilized and skeletal – of the animals found at Għar Dalam show that these were rather large animals that roamed around and therefore needed big open spaces; and that both the carnivores (meat-eating) and herbivores (vegetation-eating) presumably found what they needed. Now a tiny place like Malta could ill provide all this, even if we assume that at that time this blob of land, Malta itself, was more thickly wooded and greener than today. And we are talking here, naturally, of a time way before man made his appearance on the scene.

The appearance of man in Malta

Eventually, man appeared on earth, and, if the Olduvai Gorge finds are to be believed, man originated in Africa. Hence it is easily conceivable that the humonoid, man the nomad and hunter must also have traversed, overland from Africa into what is today known as the continent of Europe which, it bears recalling, was one land-mass interspersed in between with different-sized lakes. Before the Flood, man could have roamed the Mediterranean land-mass and that meant primitive man as well who must have also settled here. There are lots of indications that this is precisely what he did, both from the Għar Dalam remains – which show him to have been a cave-resident, and, more importantly, from the more refined constructions he left us elsewhere.

The big question mark in the minds of many is: when did Stone Age Man come to Malta? When did all this happen?

And this is where the examination of the temples, buildings and other evidence such as tools and other man-made artifacts can be of help. For wherever primitive Stone Age Man went and left behind samples of his genius in stone, he also left a legacy for future generations to try to decipher. As we have seen, the really *primitive human* must have used the natural caves that undulations in the land and the forces of nature like wind and rain and erosion had provided him. He was a cave-dweller, settling in these holes in the hill-sides that provided him with panoramic views of his hunting grounds as well as a safe haven from the vicissitudes of the weather.

As time went on, he must have learnt to excavate underground by means of primitive tools. Eventually, in a more advanced period of sophisticated calculations, he learned to build with stones held upright covered with canopies overhead.

The presence of man in Malta is marked by these gradations and in the surfeit of samples of man's handiwork that are to be found here; one finds caves, as well as underground ossuaries (hypogeums) and above-ground temples as well.

The Temples

Why did man do what he did i.e. build these huge gigantic temples in stone? And, more intriguingly, how did he do it?

In order to find the answers to some of these nagging questions we have to turn to knowledgeable archaeologists who have formulated some bold theories.

Now we know that one of the foremost archaeologists of Malta was definitely Sir Themistocles Zammit. His scientific research and his dedication to a discipline that, at the turn of the last century and beginning of this was in its infancy in Malta, have helped preserve a patrimony that would otherwise have been lost to Malta and to the world forever. He may also have helped us decipher some of the mysteries of these temples in stone to be found all over the islands.

Sir Temi Zammit worked out some theories himself. There were others, since, who proferred theirs in such a way that there has been no shortage of interpretations. We shall try to unravel some theories, which interesting and plausible though they might be, will ever remain that: theories. And we shall concentrate on one such temple area, that of **Ħaġar Qim.**

Specifically as regards Ħaġar Qim, studies made by Joseph S. Ellul following in this the line of thinking of his father who was very close to and for many years worked with Sir Temi Zammit merit attention.

Sir Temi Zammit, as a true archaeologist, would often repeat to those who would listen: **let the stones speak!** In other words one should try to figure out solutions by working on the data in-built into the stone (for which a thorough knowledge of the peculiarities of the Maltese stone is essential) rather than force one's theories on the stones and onto history. And if we do let the stones speak, we can come to a number of specific conclusions about tough questions on this particular temple complex, Ħaġar Qim.

Question 1: When was it built?

Firstly, the Ħaġar Qim complex, like all the temples of Malta and Gozo, was built during the Neolithic Age (New Stone). Ħaġar Qim took many years to build, a great number of years spanning centuries – and it must have served as a base of operations and a human settlement for these many centuries. We are lucky enough to have found on this one site the various tools that show the developmental stages of primitive man, (who as we shall see was not primitve at all) along with his mode of operation and construction.

And it is precisely by studying the mode of construction and building (*letting the stones speak*) that one realises that there is a marked developmental improvement from one section to another within this same Ħaġar Qim complex – pointing to a span of centuries in man's presence here. Such developments were brought about by improvements in the tools used – and such tool improvements did

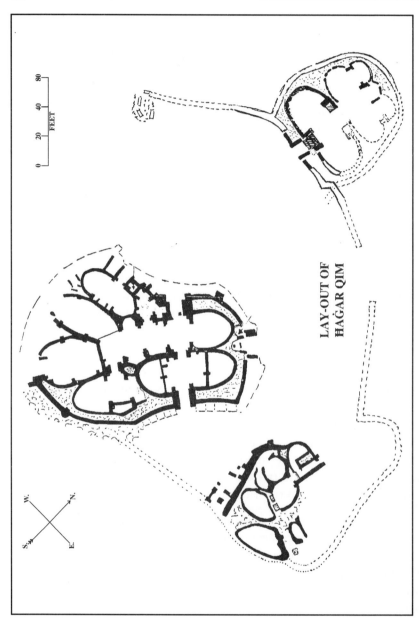

Plan of the temple complex

Aerial view (before the temple was fenced in)

not happen overnight. And so we can also come to some conclusions from the kinds of tools used.

For the kinds of tools used definitely show progressive developments that must have taken a lot of time to evolve from primitive stone instruments, for example, to those made of flint. So, at Ħaġar Qim, there must have been an *original core* building which must be the oldest because of the primitive instruments used in its construction, and then various accretions and additions in the course of time – at times over centuries – for which other types of tools were used.

The *primitive* stone implements consisted of an axe-like tool made from a wooden handle made of a solid tree branch, to which was attached the horn of a bull which is at the same time strong and flexible enough, and at the end of which a flat piece of lava was used as an adze or pick-axe as needed. (See diagram).

Lava was also used for the wheels of the carts that carried the temple-stones from the quarries to the place of construction. And if we ask where they got the lava from, the answer must be Sicily.

Communities of humans must have lived round these temples, for primitive shacks have been discovered around them as well as reservoirs for water – in Ħaġar Qim, there are seven of them; seven a magic number.

Secondly, one section of part of this complex – what must have been the original temple area, the inner sanctum – goes back some 8,000 to 10,000 years ago according to one theory. This means that man made his appearance in Malta at least that long ago – and he left us his monuments to prove it. How was this assumption arrived at?

According to Joseph S. Ellul who has given this matter deep thought and reflection and can also claim a certain familiarity with Maltese stone that only a local mason can posses, the conclusion is based on two things: a) the historicity of the biblical flood; and b) the analysis of the peculiarities of the Malta Stone.

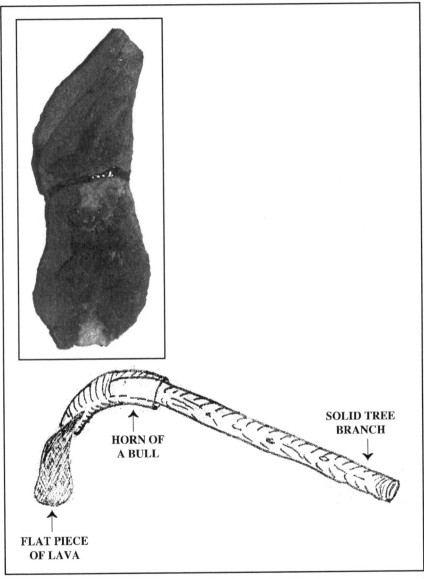

**HORN OF
A BULL**

**SOLID TREE
BRANCH**

**FLAT PIECE
OF LAVA**

Reconstruction of possible 'tool' used by early man in Malta. Inset: actual piece of lava found by J. S. Ellul

As to the flood, this was a fact that happened some 5000 years ago. This flood must have consisted of the torrential down-pours – as biblically explained in Genesis – that must have inundated whole tracts of what was previously land, and left it submerged. But accompanying the rains, there must also have been a great wave (something like a gigantic tidal wave, according to the theory explained above), which was the result of the breaching of the Atlantic Ocean at the Gibraltar-North Africa land-ridge at what is known as the Pillars of Hercules – that rippled its way from the Atlantic Ocean across the land and the lakes of that geographical area known today as the Mediterranean.

This wave came from the direction of the West going towards the East in gigantic strides. When it arrived at the land-mass in the centre of the Mediterranean linking Europe to Africa it must have hit here with great force.

It is not unthinkable, therefore, that in Malta this tidal wave-force had an effect on the temples: it not only twisted a number of these gigantic stones of the temple about in that west-east direction but it also mis-aligned others. Besides, it must have tossed some other stones quite a distance away.

As a matter of fact, when the temple was originally discovered, some temple stones were found in all three positions mentioned above – thereby confirming the conclusions proferred. Some stones were found many metres away from their original site as if tossed by some gigantic force: the great force of the tidal wave; others were found to be mis-aligned and others still, out of kilter with the rest. Some upright stone-slabs and vertical slabs on top of entrances, when the temple was first discovered, were definitely not in the original position in which they had been placed.

All of which can be taken to prove that the temples were existing before the Flood. So they are at least 5,000 years old.

But now to the more tricky part – the claim that they were

standing much longer before that. How does one come to any conclusions about it?

Answer: By following Sir Temi Zammit's advice: letting the stones speak to us. So we need to know some facts about the Malta stone.

First of all, Malta stone experts know that as regards the globigerina limestone there are several kinds but the two most important ones that concern us here are: a) the type of globigerina limestone that erodes and b) the type that does not erode. Now using these stone facts, and following the insights on the matter provided us by Joseph S. Ellul the following considerations can be made:

Type A erodes when exposed to the elements, while Type B does not erode when so exposed but on the contrary it forms a flinty skin or *patina* that hardens with the passage of time. However, if this Type B happens to have near it a stone of the Type A, it begins to erode as well.

Now studies made have shown that Type A erodes about three inches in one hundred years while Type B erodes only about a quarter inch during the same span of time. This observation holds good for all the rubble-walls around Malta, and so one can date even these same rubble-walls – if one knows how to look for these tell-tale signs and takes the trouble to work out the calculations.

As to the walls at Ħaġar Qim, the site where this phenomenon occurred was part of the third portion built in the Ħaġar Qim complex – the last portion to be built (and it must be remembered that several hundreds, if not thousands of years passed between the erection of one segment and that of another.)

At this section, then, of the Ħaġar Qim complex, the Type A eroding kind of globigerina stones exposed to the elements have eroded a thickness of about 12 inches and a quick calculation (12 inches x 4 quarters x 100 years) gives us the sum of 4,800 years.

Now when we look at the Type B globigerina stone, the noneroding stone, we find that in Ħaġar Qim there are stones which had been tossed away from the others (even as the latter remained in place) to then form the *patina* or hard crust mentioned above. Now since the huge slabs of globigerina limestone were eroded ONLY between the erection of the Temple and the collapse of the same at the flood, then adding about 5000 years from the flood-date will give us the epoch in which they were erected.

Thus, roughly, an age of 10,000 years would be a conservative estimate of the age of the original temple.

This is mind-blowing in a way and difficult to comprehend. Hence why some – among them many Maltese – find it difficult to admit that Malta could be so lucky as to have such venerable, old temples that are the oldest standing temples in the world. And so this claim based on the above reasoning is easier said than accepted especially by those who cannot imagine such a small island as Malta possessing something as precious – and as old as – in fact older than the pyramids, Stonehenge and all the other free-standing constructions in the world! All of which brings us to another point.

Question 2: How was it constructed? Could primitive man really have been so technically advanced as all this?

Having briefly touched upon the question of the age of the temples, the next logical question would be: how did these primitive peoples carry these gigantic chunks of stone, some quite bulky, and put them exactly into place, in a perfect fit?

One theory has it that these stones were partly quarried from the location itself – as has been customary in Malta ever since where builders quarry the very stones from the very building-site to then build the construction. As to the hole-in-the-ground thus created by the quarrying, the masons cover it with a roof and convert it into a deep well where water can be collected: in an arid land such wells are a thoughtful thing to have.

Some of the stones for the temple-building were also

transported from distant quarries and special bullock-drawn carts carried these stones along certain routes. A set of parallel ruts were cut into the rocky paths over which the carts traversed to create the *cart-ruts* – as these same furrows, found near temples, in different parts of the islands of Malta and Gozo, amply testify.

These very cart-ruts are further proof that in the cataclysmic flood whole chunks of land sank into the sea. Otherwise how can one explain that some of these cart-ruts end up at cliff-sides e.g. the limits of Għar Ħassan, and some are to be found on Filfla, or at Ras il-Pellegrin, right up to the cliff's edge?

The cart-ruts to be found near the Ħaġar Qim Temples further fuel the theory that the ruts led to the temples and helped in the transport of the huge slabs.

Besides the carts to transport the stones, huge and small, man must have also used wooden *sleepers* on which to roll these huge slabs and then with the huge trunks as a lever he would push them into place. The hefty stone balls that have been found in abundance in the temple precincts must have been used to manouvre the big slabs and turn them round at a corner or a bend. The purposely chipped round hollows in some of the big stones are a sure indication of this mode of carrying and putting in place. And to think that this ingenious way of tranporting was conjured up by *primitive man*.

Even granting all this, the question still remains: how did these primitive peoples, bereft of cranes and modern heavy-duty equipment, manage not only to transport but to lift these huge slabs into place? Again here, one has to consult the building and masonry stone-experts of Malta.

Mr. Joseph S. Ellul offers an ingenious solution as shown in the accompanying diagram: an inventive and creditable method by which they levered these immense stones to their upright position. Again, one must *let the stones speak* and most humbly admit that there is a lot to learn from the local stone-masons. In fact this method was

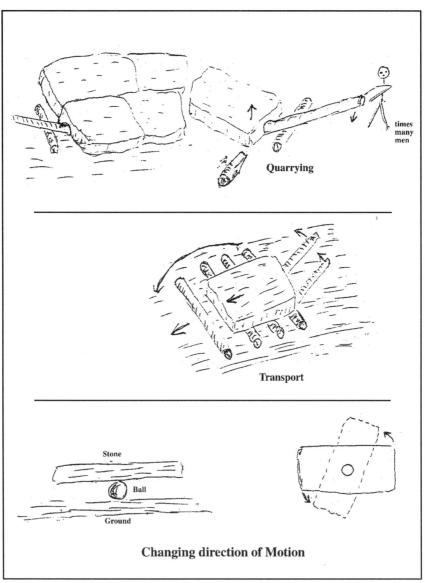

Above and opposite: How the gigantic slabs could have possibly been quarried, transported and put in place – without modern machinery

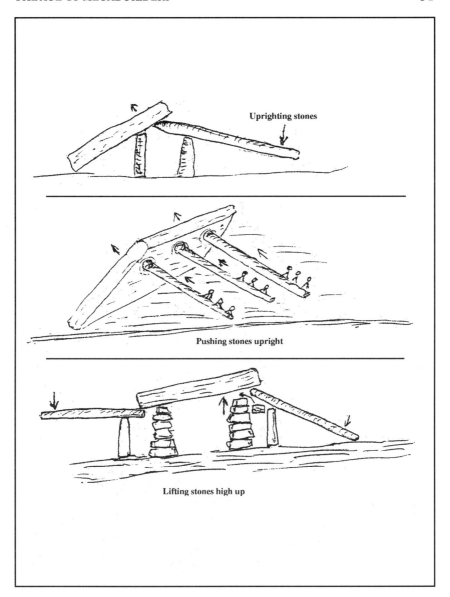

Uprighting stones

Pushing stones upright

Lifting stones high up

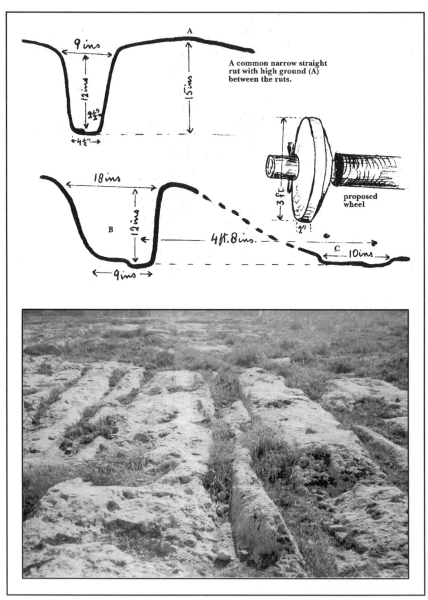

A possible explanation of the origin of the ruts

still prevalent in Malta till some time ago – before cranes killed ingenuity.

Question 3: What did these Stone People build the temples for?

As one goes around the Temples at Ħaġar Qim, Imnajdra, Ġgantija or the Hypogeum at Ħal Saflieni one cannot help but be struck by the magnificence of them all. And the question comes spontaneously to mind: Why did these people go to all this trouble?

Again, we let the stones speak. The stones, in the shape of altars, side-altars, containers to retain the sacrificial blood flowing from the altars, tethering places for sacrificial animals and such evidence give further proof that it was primitive man's desire to placate the Deity or the Deities to whom he offered sacrifices that compelled him to build these temples. They were meant for sacrificial killings and sacrifices to the gods and goddesses.

The stones also speak to us in the number of figurines portraying various gods, as well as phallic symbols. These finds which have been unearthed in the excavations give the lie to the claim that the Deity was a female fertility goddess: the *enlarged breasts* are actually enlarged male pectoral muscles, and the *female skirt* is actually the battle dress of a war-god.

As to the make-up of the temple group. First of all, there is no doubt that whole self-contained communities of human beings must have lived in huts around the temple areas since a number of wells (7 of them, the magic number 7) have also been discovered in Ħaġar Qim. As to the composition of the community: there must have been an Elder who acted as the spokesman (or priest-diviner) to offer sacrifice – for there definitely was a section where animal sacrifices were made on altars in the Holy of Holies. The blood that dripped from these altars was collected into chalice-like stone containers. Animals were also sacrificed and these must have been tethered to the hook-like holes in the slabs specially hollowed for the ropes, as they waited their turn prior to their sacrificial slaughter. They were then burnt as offerings – burnt altar stone-slabs have been found as well that inexorably point in this direction.

The reverberating incantations that re-echoed through the chambers and were magnified by means of the oracle, further added to the mystification of these sacred functions even as the women, kept segregated from the rest of the male congregation, attended the services from their appointed and separate enclosure.

All of this was indubitably connected with the various forms of worship or acts of celebration primitive man felt he had to do at different seasons of the year. For many of these temples can be called calendars in stone – accurately indicating the various solstices, equinoxes, and movements of the sun and moon within the solar system. As must have been quite natural. A community that depended on the seasons for planting and harvesting developed complicated rituals aimed at placating the deified beings called Sun and Moon – very complicated systems indeed which only today are we managing to decipher by painstaking scholarship and research.

In fact, Ħaġar Qim is a temple oriented towards the Moon and we know that the main entrance faces the rising of the full moon at its Major Standstill position while the back door opposite the main entrance faces the direction of the setting of the full moon in its northern limit at the Major Standstill. As to the Temples at Imnajdra the altar is aligned to the sun: on equinoxes, twice a year, the rising sun casts a direct light on the central altar while in the solstices, shafts of the rising sun hit through the main door on to the side-altars.

All of which alignment in both these temples could not possibly have happened accidentally.

Further evidence fuelling the theory that primitive man in Malta, (like primitive societies all over the world even today) was an *animist* is the area around the temples which shows that it served as burial grounds for the deceased. Primitive man wanted to make sure that those that departed would repose in peace and serenity without bothering too much those that had survived, the living.

The Aftermath

Confronted with all this testimony of the superhuman efforts that primitive man exerted in the construction and maintenance of such temples, the question comes to mind: How did the temple-areas degenerate to their present state of abandon? Were they deserted? Was there a cataclysmic decimation and eventual extinction of the population? How come these men built their temples in a deserted area with no vegetation around? Or was there an eventual plague that must have killed off whole settlements?

Various answers can be given, chief of which is that at the time of the construction of the temples, this area was not the kind of out-of-the-way desolation that it is today. With man and the discovery of fire and flint, we begin to witness the use of fire-wood which meant also the denudation of trees brought into the service of man for his cooking needs as well as tools for his laborious building endeavours. Even the burning of sacrificial animals must have used a lot of fire-wood, and therefore a lot of trees had to be chopped down.

This seems to be the pattern for many of the temples above ground: Ħaġar Qim, Mnajdra, Borġ in-Nadur, Ġgantija. But there are others, below ground (the *hypo-geum*) which seem to have undergone a period of desertion too.

There are many unanswered questions in this regard, and there is no doubt that the more seriously the study of archaeology is taken up in Malta, the more we are bound to come up with satisfying answers to the many questions in our minds.

It is safe to say that primitve man in Malta made a number of discoveries that have to do with the local stone and with masonry that have somehow influenced the method of building and construction in the islands ever since. The building material in the shape of stones was quarried, very often, from the building-site itself. The holes in the ground thus created were then turned into meeting-halls or wells for water storage. Centuries later, in places where a lot.

of stone had to be quarried e.g. to build some parish Churches, seeing that nothing could be built on top of the hollow ground, this area was turned into a village *piazza* or big square, with a *parvis*. Even in their time, the Knights Hospitallers would employ this same principle in the building of the New City, Valletta: holes dug in the ground to quarry the stones with which the palaces and auberges were built, were turned to stables, stores, warehouses and wells. The same economical imperatives that forced primitive man to make parsimonious use of space and material has constantly guided the masons in Malta.

As has the engineering capability of moving gigantic chunks of stone to fit them snugly into place wherever needed. This was a skill that primitve man possessed long ago and successive generations were to copy and reproduce. It is only very recently – with the introduction of earth-moving machinery in modern times – that such construction principles have been modified or flouted.

However, about those long-gone times we can say for sure that this group of little islands, which at one time were not islands at all but part of a much bigger land mass, is home to the oldest still-standing temples in the world, temples that can hold the key to many a mystery of man's arrival and sojourn on earth and his progress through the early periods of his civilizing presence – or otherwise – on earth.

Chapter 2

The Age of Phoenician Traders

(3000 B.C. to 300 B.C.)

Primitive man in Malta, as we have seen, left us many indications to prove that he was not that primitive after all. And scholarly study and patient unfolding of the mysteries surrounding the masterpieces that he left us are helping us to fathom the extent of his advanced civilization. The temples he built thousands of years ago and the artifacts he left which have come down to us are testimony to all this. It is only now that we are really beginning to try to seriously unravel it all.

Probably because of the inaccessibility of the sites, along with the fact that most of the temples were either buried underground or under tons of debris that floods, rains, alluvial deposits and such natural vicissitudes engendered, most of the archaeological wonders of pre-historic Malta were saved the visits of plundering marauders or temple-robbers. That these temples did not have anything of value in the sense of glittering baubles might have been another contributing factor to their having remained untouched.

However, all this cannot be said of the next historical period of Malta which saw the arrival of the Phoenicians and their cutural heirs, the Carthaginians. These peoples built temples and they endowed them with riches – which were sure-fire attractions to the greedy and the grabby. We know for a fact, for example, that an 'ex

An 'ex voto' candelabrum – one of two surviving

voto' candelabrum dating to this period with Phoenician and Greek inscriptions was presented to Louis XIV of France by Grand Master Manoel de Rohan. At present this candelabrum is to be found at the Louvre in Paris.

Luckily, it was not a unique sample. Another candelabrum that was saved such honorific generosity at other people's expense is still to be found in Malta – to grace the local Museum of Archaeology.

How did the Phoenicians end up in Malta and what influence has their presence had on Malta?

The origin of the Phoenicians and Carthaginians

First of all the Phoenicians were the descendants of the Canaanites going back to the 3rd. millenium B.C whose origins are unknown but who had settled in Byblos, Sidon and Tyre (sites in modern-day Lebanon). The Egyptians had a word for them: *fenkhw* which meant Asiatics. The Bible calls them equally Sidonians and Tyrians. Homer calls them *phoinikos* probably because of their blood-red skin colour. We know also that in Hebrew, *kena'ani* (from which: canaanite) has the secondary meaning of tradesmen – and that indeed they were, for they journeyed all over the Mediterranean buying and selling their wares.

By the 2nd millenium, the Phoenicians had travelled to the Levant to Joppa, Dor and such places, and abroad to Ugarit. By the 15th century B.C. they had extended their influence to Utica in North Africa and probably Cadiz (Spain) as well.

By 900 B.C. they had established trading posts in the Mediterranean including Carthage (in modern-day Tunisia) and by about 600 B.C. they had gone even further. They are even said to have circumnavigated Africa.

It is known that along the Mediterranean the Phoenicians must have established several smaller settlements such as Campas, Cossyra (modern-day Pantelleria), Gaulos (Gozo) and Melita (Malta) –

though only in the latter place, Malta, have Phoenician remains going back to the 7th century B.C. been found.

The Phoenicians journeyed, venturing where no humans had done before and their transactions included such material as linen, metal, glass, wood, ivory, gold, silver and precious stones. But they were not just traders: they were a civilized and civilizing lot, and are said to have invented the modern alphabet as well.

When the Phoenicians began to wane, their economic, cultural and spiritual descendants, the Carthaginians, took over. As such the latter set up an empire over the old Phoenician settlements. These Carthaginians were called *Punic* by the Romans, an adjective derived from *Poeni* – the Latin name for the Greek *phoinikos* – phoenician. The Romans fought long-drawn out wars with them spanning more than a hundred years until at last in 146 B.C. Scipio Jr. destroyed Carthage and declared Africa a Roman colony. (Later, Carthage was to regain prominence and pride of place as a centre of Christianity – as well as notoriety as the breeding-ground of the Donatist heresy.)

Phoenician commerce

The Phoenicians were traders who plied the Mediterranean from their homeland (modern Lebanon), all the way to Cadiz in Spain and Tangier in North Africa, thus touching on the main ports of the then known world which was co-terminous with the Mediterranean Basin.

The safe and sheltered havens of Malta must have provided some respite to these people on their long and difficult journeys. Malta must have provided as well a *warehousing depot* where they could temporarily store their many goods in textiles, ceramics, terracotta and ivory. Indeed some hold that the name Malta originates from the Phoenician word *malat* which means shelter.

Materials dating to these times have been found at the various havens in Malta known to be of Phoenician origin namely: Għajn Qajjet (Rabat) and Tas-Silġ (Marsaxlokk). The latter was probably also a holy site where a temple must have stood: figurines were found here which represent the deity Tanit.

We are lucky to have even this much as testimony of the Phoenician presence in these islands besides the tombs. Apart from the rapaciousness and/or callousness of subsequent rulers of Malta (example: Grand Master de Rohan above), there was another factor: their main trade was in perishable goods such as textiles. On top of it all, they were not in the habit of establishing 'colonies' wherever they cast anchor, where fellow-nationals would be appointed as local guardians to keep an eye on the goods.

Even then, they must have made an exception in Malta, due to the mildness of the climate here and the natural protection the local harbours offered to their sailing-boats especially during the winter months. Added to which was the fact that these islands were strategically placed half-way across the Mediterranean – and the Phoenician trade-route.

The Carthaginians

However, powerful as they were and far-flung as much as their empire was, as often happens in history, their power had to reach a zenith – and begin to wane. Waiting in the wings were the Carthaginians whose origins too are shrouded in mystery or at least in epic poems. The legend in Virgil's *Aeneid* has it that a Tyrian princess of Tyre, fleeing from her brother Pygmalion (the name of a historical king in Tyre) eventually settled in North Africa (in Carthage). In time these immigrant settlers became a powerful empire that would even threaten and take on mighty Rome. The Carthaginians expanded to Sardinia and Sicily and hence made their appearance in Malta and, in a natural take-over of power (*pacifica possessio*) from the waning Phoenicians, Malta too passed into the hands of the new sea-power, the Carthaginians.

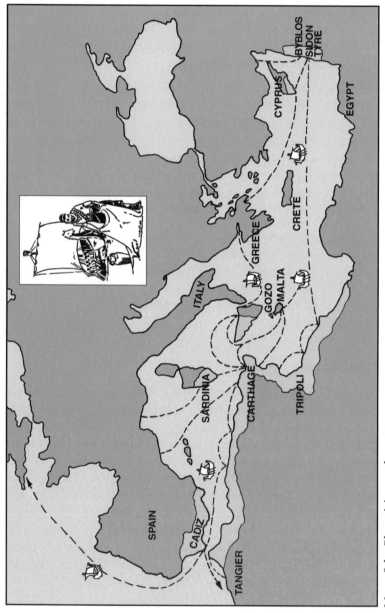

Map of the Phoenician trade route

In Malta, the Carthaginians set about establishing the forms of government modelled on the Greek States. They also set about building their temples which, if Roman historians and orators are to be believed, were quite a sight to behold. As to the local people, they were employed in weaving multi-coloured silk products and cloths and long tunics for the women. Coral was also harvested and honey was cultivated.

The Carthaginians are credited with having introduced the carob tree. The fruit of the latter served not only as horse fodder but for the making of a kind of carob-syrup (produced to this day). Mention is also made at this time of the pedigree Maltese dog.

Religious worship

These Middle Eastern peoples must have established their religion in Malta as well. We know that the principal gods that they worshipped were El, Baal (which means: My Lord and Master). The Phoenicians however joined their god Echmun (dubbed Aesculapius by the Romans) to a consort called Anat (changed to Tanith in Carthage) and who in her virgin form was worshipped as Astharte – Ashtart.

Bronze coins sculpted in characters which are Punic-hellenic-roman have been found dating back to this period. As is to be expected images of the gods these people worshipped are engraved on these coins. Statues, tombs, amphorae, water-containers, and oil-lamps dating back to this time have also been found.

However, as was hinted earlier, the most precious historical fragment that remains of this period is the candelabrum-base, an 'ex voto' (vow made to a divinity in exchange for some favour requested or received), which has an inscription in Phoenician and Greek and which therefore was of help in the deciphering of the Phoenician language.

This reads: "To Melchart, Lord of the City of Tyre, Abdasar

along with his brother Aserkemor, made this pledge; both sons of Asirxehor son of Abdasar, may he (Melchart) hearken to their words and bless them."

It may be of interest to note that although at the time of the offering of the candelabrum Malta was bi-lingual (Phoenician and Greek), by the year 40. B.C. Latin substituted the Phoenician language and eventually Greek became the *lingua franca* among the ruling classes.

Phoenician-Carthaginian influences

As to the Phoenicians and the Carthaginians (i.e. the Canaanites), their penchant for trading and doing business – which took them literally to the ends of the earth – is well-known in ancient history. The trading skills of these peoples were passed on to the inhabitants of that land called Lebanon who are known for their business acumen even to this day.

No doubt, the Maltese dealing with such skillful tradesmen must have learnt a trick or two from them and sharpened their own business acumen accordingly. This is one of the traits from the Phoenicians that the Maltese must have received, copied and retained to this day, for the Maltese can strike a good bargain. They also make enterprising tradesmen.

The other Phoenician bequest to Malta was the language – though this is a hotly argued point among local linguistic scholars. There are those who argue that present-day Maltese owes its origin to and is a direct descendant of Phoenician. There are others that question it all.

What cannot be questioned is one Phoenician bequest that the Maltese have inherited and that is the love of adventure especially where the glory of sea-faring and sea-lore is concerned. The Maltese make good sailors and are to be found on board of many ships plying the sea-lanes of the world.

Finally, it may be a bit far-fetched to say but the various cultural and religious over-lays that various civilizations brought to Malta must have had an influence on the outlook of the local population as well. Among these is the in-bred characteristic of the Maltese psyche which can accommodatingly adapt to foreigners, their customs, their religious beliefs as well as their idiosyncracies. The seeds for some of this must have been planted under the Phoenicians and the Carthaginians. It is well-known that the Maltese have learnt the art of survival – by learning to adapt. And the Phoenicians must have been among the first to teach this art to the Maltese. In fact, if, as has been hinted, some Phoenicians did end up settling in Malta, they might have been the first teachers of this very important trait that was to stand the Maltese so well throughout their history of domination by successive foreign powers. As we shall have plenty of occasion to see as the centuries unfold and the various layers of history are peeled off.

Chapter 3

The Age of Roman Emperors and Pauline Shipwrecks

(3rd Cent B.C. to 4th cent A.D.)

History shows us that even as one super-power starts waning, another is waiting in the wings, or better still has already started making waves, ready and willing to take over. Now it was the turn of that new nation called Rome to dominate the Mediterranean Basin. Not that this happened overnight. The Romans as a people took 500 years to build their empire, conquering new territories on the way or, mostly, those already belonging to someone else. As we have seen, it took them more than a century to dominate that other super-power, the Punics (Phoenician-Carthaginians). But Rome waged these wars and her historians glorified the deeds in what have come to be known as the Punic Wars: First and Second and Third.

And Rome waged more wars still, to conquer France this time. This came to be known as the 'Gallic War'. A historian wrote about it – glowing memoirs from the very general who led the campaign, Julius Caesar. And Rome waged more wars still: to the north and south of her, to the east and the west of her – and conquered more territories until it became an immense empire. And somewhere in the midst of this expansive empire there was a tiny colony called Melita.

It is not certain whether Malta fell to the Romans during the first or the second campaign to unseat the Punics from the island.

What is certain is that during the Second Punic War, the local Carthaginian representative in Malta, by the name of Hamilcar, son of Gisko, along with the commander of the local garrison surrendered to the Roman Consul Titus Sempronius Longus. Truth to tell the Roman Consul had proved a formidable assailant in Syracuse, having devastated Hiero, the local governor there along with his defences before coming to Malta in 218 B.C.

With such formidable credentials on the Consul's side, Hamilcar son of Gisko must have thought it the better part of valour to avoid useless bloodshed and massacre, and so surrender he did. Eventually, in the ruthless laws of warfare of the time where winner takes all and the devil take the hindmost, Hamilcar and his whole Carthaginian entourage ended up as prisoners to be eventually sold as slaves in the market at Marsala (in Sicily).

This victory put the seal on Malta as part of the new mighty Roman Empire which at this time was busy consolidating its claim to an undisputed domain in the Mediterranean and beyond, and which meant establishing a centralized form of government by imposing the one true Roman religion within the Hellenic-Roman culture, building a communications net-work that is a marvel to this day and strengthening the Roman gold 'denar' to make it the only form of currency, thus facilitating commercial exchanges. (Echos of Euro, the European Currency Unit – which the European Union in our 20th century wants to adopt as the monetary unit common to all the member states).

Henceforth, therefore, Malta could come in handy, with its strategic position in the middle of the Mediterranean, as a base in further campaigns especially against those Punics who would not take things lying down and would fan smouldering embers to try to work up a conflagration that would revolt against Roman tyranny.

Malta, again because of its safe harbours and geographical situation at the centre of the then-known world, the Mediterranean, must have served as a convenient base for the punitive campaigns as well as adventurous forays that the Roman legions felt duty-bound to undertake to Carthage to the south. However, as the Roman Empire became stronger, there were less and less threats from the western Mediterranean, and the importance of Malta as a base and as an *entrepot* (storage place) diminished.

As time went on and the local *barbarians*, especially those with Punic sympathies, learned to appreciate Roman culture and religion and civilization, these latter civilizing influences became better established locally as well – with the construction of temples to Juno (Venus) such as the one at Dejr Limara and to Prosperina (the goddess of wheat, daughter of Ceres) at Imtarfa. Eventually the Roman pagan religion was so well entrenched that we even find Maltese women who attained the rank of *flamines* or temple priestesses.

We know all this because Malta for a time had a Praetor (appointed by Rome) by the name of Caius Verres. He was one of the worst that could be assigned to this god-forsaken outpost – a civil servant who definitely gave the Roman colonial policy a bad name in these islands. So much so that he was vilified and his foul deeds exposed in the Roman Senate by none other than the Quaestor and famous Orator, Marcus Tullius Cicero – who is reputed to have visited the island (one of a never-ending series of famous men and women who were so to grace these shores).

In Cicero's speeches titled *In Caium Verrem* we have wonderful vignettes about life in contemporary Malta and about the kind of work the people did (weaving of colourful cloth as material for women's dresses – a carry-over industry from Phoenician times). But let us hear what Cicero himself has to say in the fourth book, his Second Speech against Verres:

"The island of Melita, gentlemen, is separated from Sicily by a rather wide and dangerous stretch of sea. In it there is a town, also called Melita, which Verres never visited, but which nonetheless he turned for three years into a factory for the weaving of women's dresses. On a headland not far from the town stands an ancient temple of Juno, which has ever been held in such reverence that its sanctity has not once been violated not only in the old days of the Punic Wars, the naval operation of which took place in and around this region, but even by pirate hordes of our own days. Nay, there is also the story of how King Masinissa's fleet once put in there, and the king's admiral carried off from the shrine some ivory tusks of astonishing size, conveyed them to Africa, and presented them to Masinissa. At first, the king was delighted with the gift; but presently, when he was told where they came from, he dispatched a chosen body of men in a large warship to restore the tusks to their place; and upon the tusks was engraved an inscription in Punic characters, recording how king Masinissa had received them unwittingly, and on learning the truth had ordered them to be brought back and re-installed in place. Besides these tusks there was a great quantity of ivory, and many objects of art, including some ivory figures of [the goddess] Victory, of ancient and exquisite workmanship. Well, to omit details, one attempt, one message was enough for Verres' purpose: by means of temple slaves dispatched for the purpose, he had every one of these treasures removed and carried away.

In the name of the gods, what manner of man am I prosecuting? … The representatives of the people of Melita state officially that the temple of Juno has been robbed, that Verres has left nothing behind in that most holy sanctuary; that the place where our friends have often landed and the pirates are in the habit of passing winter after winter, without any pirate's ever desecrating it or any enemy's laying hands upon it – this place has now been so thoroughly robbed by Verres that nothing has been left there."

So much for Cicero.

In their more than seven hundred years' presence in Malta and once the obeisance of the populace was fully established, the Romans progressively gave more and more autonomy to the Maltese. We cannot, however, say that Malta was a *foederata civitas*, a federated i.e. incorporated city-state, with all the rights and privileges that such a status entailed. At most it must have been a *civitas sine foedere libera*: a free city without federation. As such it had only to pay taxes and not the slavery-tariffs. In fact it was considered *demanialis* i.e. governed by Rome.

Luckily not every Praetor or *Primus Omnium* (i.e. the Foremost – the title the Acts of the Apostles applies even to Publius, who was the Chief in Malta) that governed Malta were of the Caius Verres type. Some governors were better than others. After all there was a thriving community of Romans in Malta and they deserved good governors. That there was such a thriving community of Romans in Malta is evidenced by the many testimonies they left behind: the Roman *domus* at Rabat with the mosaic *peristylium* in the centre to hold the rain water; the marble statues – some of which, like the head of Tiberius, still in a good state of preservation; the *thermae* at Għajn Tuffieħa complete with baths with hot and cold water as well as the *hypocaustum*, a water-heating room. There are also such things as wells, tombs, amphorae, coins and even statues including those of gods and goddesses – to mention just a few of the many Roman remains in Malta.

Of special interest is the slab to be found in Gozo recording the collection made among the local people for the erection of a statue to Marcus Vallius. The inscription shows that even as of this time, Gozo was a Roman *municipium* already. All of the above shows that in their many centuries' sojourn in these islands the Romans brought with them their beliefs, their temples, their gods and goddesses as well as their language and their culture.

The Romans had risen to sovereignty over the world, in the Mare Nostrum and beyond, by sheer military genius – a disciplined and ruthless army, mostly made up of mercenaries, under capable generals that established a little bit of Rome wherever they could. As such a *Primus Omnium* or Praetor was the local Head or Governor,

Sample of Roman mosaic to be found in Rabat (Malta)

The Roman Baths at Għajn Tuffieħa

a Roman, representing the might of Rome locally and having absolute power because he was answerable only to Rome.

The Malta governor may have actually resided here or, probably as happened most of the time, in Sicily. Under him must have been the people that helped in the government: the *Curia* which saw to the due execution of bureaucratic red-tape.

A big enough chunk of land called *municipium* could even be accorded a Governor's representative on the spot to take care of administrative affairs locally. Under this system of government and colonial management, Malta and its sister island Gozo must have thrived as they formed part of the mighty Roman Empire.

However, even as the Roman presence in Malta was at its highest after more than two hundred years' sojourn here, Destiny had another surprise in store for these islands in the shape of a V.I.S. (Very Important Saint) of the first order whose arrival to the shores of Malta was to change the course of its history as no other event had done to date – and as no other would ever do in the future.

That fact was the shipwreck, one wintry night, of St Paul on the island that the Romans now called *Melita* – the land of honey.

A Christian Interlude in Pagan Malta: The Shipwreck of Paul

In his 'Acts of the Apostles' (Chap. 27, 28), St Luke says:

"When day broke they could not make out the land; but they noticed a bay with a beach, and they proposed to run the ship ashore there if they could. So they slipped the anchors and committed themselves to the sea, at the same time unlashing the fastenings of the rudders; and hoisting the foresail to the breeze, they made for the beach. But we struck a place open to two seas, and they ran the ship aground. The prow stuck fast and remained immovable, but the stern began to break up under the the violence of the sea. Now the solders planned to kill the prisoners lest any of them should swim ashore and escape, but the centurion, wishing to save Paul, put a stop to their plan. He ordered those who could swim to jump overboard first and get to land, and they brought the rest in, some on planks and others on various pieces from the ship. And so it came to pass that all got safely to land.

After our escape we learned that the island was called Malta. And the natives showed us no little kindness, for they kindled a fire and refreshed us all because of the rain that had set in, and the cold. Now Paul gathered a bundle of sticks and laid them on the fire, when a viper came out because of the heat and fastened on his hand. When the natives saw the creature hanging from his hand, they said to one another, 'Surely this man is a murderer, for though he has escaped the sea, Justice does not let him live.' But he shook off the creature into the fire and suffered no harm. Now they were expecting that he would swell up and suddenly fall down and die; but after waiting a long time and seeing no harm come to him, they changed their minds and said that he was a god.

Now in the vicinity there were estates belonging to the head man of the island, whose name was Publius, and he received us and entertained us hospitably for three days. And it happened that the father of Publius was laid up with fever and dysentery; but Paul went in, and after praying and laying his hands on him, he healed him. After this all the sick on the island came and were cured; and they honoured us with many marks of honour, and when we sailed, they provided us with such things as we needed.

We set sail after three months in an Alexandrian ship with the Twins on her figurehead, which had wintered at the island."

One would think that even the most meticulous and wary of biblical scholars and exegetes would look at this text and conclude without a shadow of a doubt that St Paul, Roman citizen that he claimed to be, on his way to stand trial in Rome, was shipwrecked on an island called Melita. Here, as the biblical narrative plainly states, he sojourned for three months enjoying the islands' traditional hospitality and in turn making christians of all of them. In fact, in Malta there is even a little group of islands called **Il-Gżejjer ta' San Pawl** (the Islands of St Paul) to mark the exact traditional spot where the shipwreck took place.

As a result of this belief in St Paul's shipwreck and sojourn here, the Maltese have ever since claimed apostolic origins for their brand of Christianity and the Apostle Paul as the (Spiritual) Father of the Nation.

You would think that with all this going for them, Malta and the Maltese would be acknowledged as the true spiritual heirs of this Apostle of the Gentiles who changed the face of gentile, and at the time Roman pagan, Malta.

But no! Much to the chagrin of some Maltese, a number of modern so-called scriptural exegetes have to go and mess around with irrefragable scriptural proof abetted by a well-established tradition to place the **Melita of the Acts** elsewhere than in Malta, in the West Grecian Sea. In Cephallonia as a matter of fact! And St Paul to have converted another Melita altogether!

All this because of the unlikelihood of the existence of poisonous vipers on the Maltese islands and the improbability that a *grigale* no matter how violent or stormy could have carried Paul and his captors so far off course from the previous port of call, which must have probably been Crete.

The Maltese people, of course, do not take kindly to anybody messing around with their reading of history – which after all is a very scriptural reading of history as found in the Acts of the Apostles. They would hear of none of this twisting of scriptural texts and they believe today, as they have believed for two thousand odd years, that St Paul brought the Christian faith to Malta and established the local Christian Church here. At least those of the Maltese who still

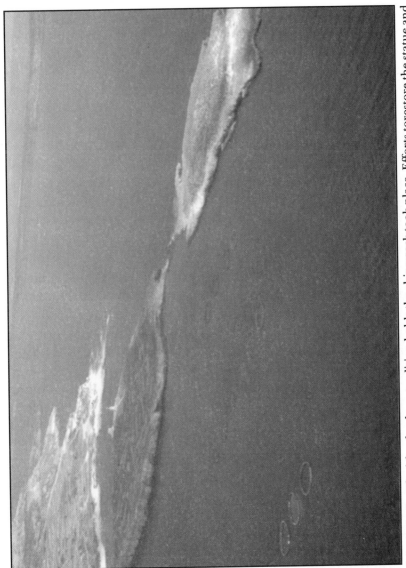

"Il-Gżejjer" – The islands where tradition holds the shipwreck took place. Efforts to restore the statue and site are at hand by "Din l-Art Ħelwa"

believe in Christianity, and a certified number of those who do not, would read history this way.

But more than this. There are those who will go further and, in keeping with long-standing tradition, aver to the fact that St Paul appointed the local representative of the Roman Empire who by Roman law was already the Governor or Head or *Primus Omnium* and whose name was Publius, as the first bishop of Malta. By Roman administrative law he was already the First Citizen within the Roman colonial system on the island anyhow.

Very probably Publius was not a native-born Maltese but a true-blooded Roman patiently biding his time at this Roman Empire outpost, forsaken by the gods, waiting for a peachier assignment in appreciation of faithful service and unquestioning obedience within a pyramidal civil service.

But then Paul and his entourage along with his Roman captors had to be shipwrecked on the island and the course of Maltese history was changed. So was the career of the Governor Publius.

From a country of pagans with their own gods and believers wallowing in ancestral worship and led by *flamines*, as the temples extant from contemporary Malta show, the local natives were converted to Christianity. True, all this could not have happened suddenly and overnight but over a period of time. In fact, during the three months that Paul was on the island, he must have been kept pretty busy catechizing and evangelizing and baptizing the Elders of Malta as well as members of the local population which at that time must have amounted to a few thousands, mostly living in the capital city on a hill at Rabat.

As Paul did everywhere else he went and as he tells us in most of the Epistles he wrote to the other Christian Churches, he must have established the local Church in Malta as well with the various ministers that catered to the various functions and needs, spiritual and material, of the local populace, most probably complete with deacons and deaconesses. Tradition has it that in all this, fellow-companion and Apostle Luke gave quite a helping hand and there is even a painting of the Madonna in Mellieħa, purported to be Luke's handiwork, to prove it.

Historically we know very little about this particular period of history because so little evidence has remained except in legend or word-of-mouth traditions purportedly passed on from one generation to the next, most of which did not necessarily originate with the Pauline period in Malta. Such Pauline legends were to receive special encouragement later under the Hospitallers for we know that their anti-Moslem animosity was dead set against even the least non-Christian influence on the islands. And what better way to do this than by fostering Pauline-Christian legends, even such of questionable provenance, as long as they helped to re-inforce the true apostolic origin of the faith in Malta? And what harm in lending a hand by inventing a legend or two about Paul's presence here?

Hence the reason why some would question whether the Pauline traditions really go back that far, to the times of St Paul and immediately afterwards, or rather to the Knights Hospitallers. It is always difficult to sift objective truth from popular legend in such traditions.

For most Maltese, of course, the narration of events as found in the Acts of the Apostles, whose authorship is assigned to another close disciple of Christ, the Apostle Luke, is more than enough evidence for a faith that is, in popular tradition again, as strong as the rock upon which both Malta and Gozo are sited. Even though Luke paid the Maltese no compliment by calling the native Maltese *barbarians* – though this is explained away by saying that in those times barbarians were those who did not speak that civilizing tongue called Greek. And who can blame the Greek-speaking elite for being so snobbish?

The Aftermath of Paul's visit

As a result of modern scholarly scrutiny of ancient traditions, there is one such pauline tradition that comes under close examination.

And that is the one which sees the whole population of the Maltese Islands convert to Christianity as a result of Paul's visit to Malta and his three months' sojourn here.

Such enthusiasm for apostolic wonders, though by no means beyond the pale of miraculous powers, must be mitigated by the fact that in these islands there were pagan temples dedicated to the Roman gods (Apollo, Hercules, Prosperina, Juno/Venus) that remained open for the veneration and worship of the faithful long after Paul left Malta. In fact there are reports that certain embellishments and repairs to such temples were made well into the end of the first century i.e. well after Paul's visit here.

We also find names in epigraphs in both Malta and Gozo of *flamines*, the pagan priests who ministered in the Roman temples here, as well as descriptions of generous donations made by the population of the Municipium of Malta for the building of an altar to Apollo and the marble flooring of the temple along with a *parvis* and crypt for same and the erection of a statue.

Now all this could not have happened were it not for the fact that a sizeable number of the local population were still followers of the pagan Roman religion. And these contributors could not all have been foreign settlers from Rome.

It is difficult to re-construct what happened in the aftermath of the Apostle Paul's visit to Malta. Very probably the two religions, the Roman pagan and the Pauline Christian co-existed one alongside the other. There is no trace of any persecution of Christians, as was the case in Rome. But there the new subversive Christian religion was viewed as a threat to Rome and its position of authority and wealth in the then known world. There the threat was felt because this new religion, the Christian faith, wanted to substitute the old Roman pantheon with the new Trinitarian Divinity. Again, the teaching that considered all humans, whether freemen or bondsmen, whether slaves or free, equal in the sight of a Loving Father, must have been seen as very much of a threat to an empire that

St Paul's Shipwreck Church, Valletta dressed up for the occasion

survived on slavery and thrived on autocratic and imperial repression.

Be that as it may, the problems that early Christianity faced in Rome were, apparently, unknown in Malta. From all appearances, in fact, the Roman Empire thrived and flourished and co-existed with Christianity in Malta. It is also very probable that the Christian Church adopted the Roman system and mode of government in its administrative aspects. The title **the Roman** Church was and has remained more than a title in Malta: it was an adaptation of the administrative system of pagan Rome.

However, the Roman Empire had had its day. As the lessons of history constantly teach us, an empire even one as well-knit and autocratic as the Roman, could not last forever. It was truly a far-flung empire. But even this mighty empire started crumbling and as it waned, another was starting its ascendancy: it was now the turn of the Goths and the Vandals, those savage barbarians from the North to take over.

Why did the Roman Empire collapse? Various theories have been offered for its decline. Whatever the reason for the Romans' demise, be it the easy life that had turned them to flabby and corrupt imperialists bent solely on the pleasures of the flesh, or be it the fact that like all empires, the time of its decline had come because the very extent of it all made it difficult to protect and defend with wars bleeding its treasury, the fact remains that Rome's time was up. And they who had ruled in glory over the then known world, the Mediterranean, from the Middle Eastern countries of Palestine and Syria, all over North Africa and Europe right up to Britain and Scotland, were now no more a force to be reckoned with.

Their communications and roads system (that is a marvel to contemplate even these many hundreds of years later) could not save them from their destiny at the hands of the Vandals and the Goths. Neither could their culture, language and system of government be saved from the savagery of the next invaders of

Europe. If anything, the Vandals and Goths were more ruthless and iron-handed than even the Romans themselves. They were to ravage and ransack and pillage and destroy whatever the Romans had painstakingly built over the centuries in what has come to be known as a reign of terror and tyranny.

Fortunately the Vandals' reign of terror did not reach Malta; at least we do not have any records of their presence here. Fortunately too, their dominion was not to last long. In the wake of the devastation of the Vandals and Goths who were more bent on destroying than building and over the ashes of what they had destroyed, a new empire was to be built as the Emperor Constantine came on the scene – which brings us to another chapter in Malta's long history.

Chapter 4

The Age of Byzantine Intrigues

(4th to the 8th centuries A.D.)

By the fourth century of the New Era, (the Christian Era was only later to be known as A.D: Anno Domini), the Emperor Constantine had made Christianity the official religion of his new Byzantine Empire that now officially superseded all the others before him.

Under the Emperor Constantine, the balance of power in the Mediterranean – which made up, at this time, much of what was known of the whole world – shifted from Rome to Constantinople. This city was now officially called the **New City** by the new emperor, to distinguish it from the old. Thus the centre of the new empire shifted from Latin Rome *eastwards* to Greek Constantinople.

And a whole new civilization and mode of government was launched.

In this, Constantine's purported visionary appearances from heaven prophesying his great victories for the faith by the sign of the Cross must have played an important part. At least they must have been seen to give heavenly inspiration and approval to the Constantinian shift of power from West to East, from Rome to Constantinople.

As far as the islands of Malta and Gozo were concerned, they too must have passed into the hands of Byzantium even though they went through a scary period when first Genseric, head of the Vandals and then the Goths became lords and masters of all they surveyed and conquered in their drive southwards that took them as far as the Sicilian possessions and North Africa. And since the destiny of the Maltese Islands was linked with that of Sicily, the Maltese could not escape the fate that befell the Sicilians. It must be admitted, though, that there is little historical evidence for any hard-nosed conclusions about the presence of Vandals or Goths in Malta – all of which must therefore remain in the realm of conjecture.

Nor do we have much evidence of what Malta was like under the Byzantines who, having subjugated the Vandals and the Goths, ruled the Mediterranean for the next many centuries – and were in Malta for about four hundred years. There is periodic mention of Malta as a stop-over place for the punitive forces making their way to quell some Goth or Vandal insurrection here and there in North Africa or Sicily, and therefore with their sailing ships seeking refuge in these protected harbours. But apart from that, there is nothing much of any importance or value during the Byzantine Era in Malta.

For the Byzantines, administratively, Malta and Gozo were grouped with the regional sub-division that included Sicily, the Basilicata, Calabria and Puglia. Hence the Maltese Islands were an insignificant group of little islands, a small colony at best overshadowed by the bigger provinces. Yet Malta must have had the same Code of Laws as the rest of the Byzantine Empire.

The Byzantines followed the laws formulated in the Justinian Code, and in keeping with this code, a region was placed in the charge of the *Praetor* i.e. Civil Governor. Some writings speak of just such a governor of Sicily *and the other islands* – which must refer to Malta and Gozo and Pantelleria.

The local representative of the Empire in a colony was embodied in the *Dux*, a sort of Garrison Chief entrusted with the defence; in the case of the islands, the defence of Malta and Gozo. He was answerable to the *Magister Militum per orientem* – the Head of the Army of the East.

Falconry has always been a favourite sport in Malta

As far as religion was concerned, under the Byzantines, the Greek ritual and language for services must have been used. For a time, the previous ritual in (Roman) Latin or other languages must have been tolerated and allowed to be used *pari passu* – for such previous rituals, equally Christian though in that barbaric tongue Latin, could not have been totally and radically abrogated or supplanted.

But eventually, as happens with colonies everywhere, the language, customs and rituals of the conquerors were adopted partly because they were considered superior by the natives and therefore their adoption also a measure of sophisticated imitation of the more cultured foreigner, and partly because the cultured foreigner would not demean himself by going native.

Malta as part of this new Holy Christian Byzantine Empire must have followed the traditions adopted everywhere else, including Rome, at times even by Edict. The Edict of Theodosius empowered new Churches of this new faith to be built over the sites and from the dismantled material of the old sites (especially pagan Roman sites) to show the eradication of the latter and the total domination of the former. In the process much of the evidence and many of the traces of what had gone before were obliterated.

In this period various Christian symbols like the fish (ixthus), the palm, the deer, pea-cock and the cross make their appearance in Malta and Gozo. Traces of same are to be found as well as remains of what must have originally been a basilica with a rectangular-shaped baptistry and an altar in the middle.

Henceforth, Christianity was the official religion of the Byzantine Empire and so had the upper hand. Hence the pains of persecution that Christians had suffered under the Roman pagans (mostly in Rome), could now be inflicted on all those who did not embrace this new faith of this new empire. In fact, in a reversal of roles, refusal to accept the new faith was often punished by beheading and so it is not surprising that many subjects opted for conversion. This policy must have been followed in Malta and hence the reason why some historians believe that the Maltese population turned totally towards Christianity at this time rather than at Paul's time.

The particularly *byzantine* problems that simmered in Greek Christianity must have made their way to Malta as well, specifically the monophysite controversy (whether in the one person of Christ there is one nature or two: the divine and/or human) and the iconoclastic controversy (whether the images of Christ and the saints can and should be venerated in Christian Churches) and such debates.

Historical references are made in passing that provide bits of information about daily life in these islands. Of particular interest was the case presented to and brought to judgment before Pope Gregory I (the Great) whereby the local bishop of Malta, a certain Lucillus along with his son Peter were accused of embezzling funds and misusing Church property. They were brought to court before John, Bishop of Syracuse. They were found guilty and forced to refund all stolen funds and property, even as Bishop Lucillus was further punished and deprived of his See for such improper behaviour unbecoming of a head of a Church.

Another curious event for which Malta may have in time acquired the unhappy reputation of being a *penal colony and refuge for rejects from other nations* was that in the 7th century, the Moslem Chief Ambr-ibn-asi who had captured Cyrenaica and the Pentapolis (the five satellite cities) as well as Tripoli (with its famous Sabrath and Leptis Magna) negotiated with the Patriarch of Constantinople for the release of the captive Byzantine Christians of those places. By mutual agreement between the Patriarch and Ambr-ibn-asi it was arranged to have these refugees re-settled in the Maltese Islands. Naturally this influx of immigrants *from the east and North Africa* besides giving Malta, unjustifiably, the unsavoury reputation mentioned above, must have also been instrumental in further influencing the language and culture of the islands in its semitic roots.

All in all, though, it is a pity that about this rather extensive period of the Byzantine presence in Malta we have very little historical information. One probable reason is that the invaders and rulers that next came to Malta were the Moslem Arabs who, with their strict penchant for removing all *craven images* in the shape of paintings or statues must have made a clean sweep of that favourite Byzantine distinguishing trait: their love for and abundance of icons and images. And with the customary attendant colonial policy, on the part of the Moslem Arabs now, of building the new places of worship on the site of the previous places of worship, much of what had been constructed before must have been demolished, to be superseded by the new culture. Thus we are to believe that a number of mosques were built over what formerly had been Byzantine Churches. Hence, as such, much of what the Byzantine presence in Malta must have achieved will never be known even though much of the research about this period has still to be done.

We can only surmise, conjecture and try to re-construct.

It must be great to think that among the educated elite in these islands, the common language was Greek; that most any Christian services that were held were in the Greek Byzantine rite; and that even the subtle and not so subtle nuances that Christian theology took in the form of christological beliefs (the nature of Christ) and form of worship (to icons/images/statues etc.) were all leaning towards the Byzantine traditions.

Indeed we have some teasing examples of faint traces of Greek in the Maltese language that might be said to have come from this Byzantine period: *Lapsi* is the Maltese word for the Ascension of Christ into Heaven and this may have come from the Greek word for the same feast, Analepsis. The sacrament of the anointing of the Sick was known as Miru; while the sacrament of baptism is still called *magħmudija*; the Maltese word for money *flus* seems to be a corruption of the Greek word *obolos* which the Byzantines themselves corrupted into *follis*.

Malta has retained its Greek connection. The Greek Catholic Church boasts of an icon of Our Lady of Damascus that goes back to the 11th century. The Greek Orthodox too have a church in Valletta

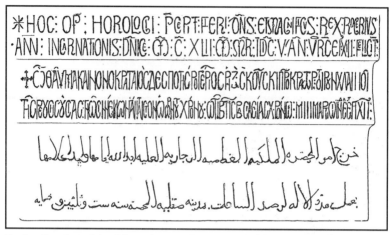

Latin, Greek and Arabic script recalling the Maltese watchmaker

The Byzantine Empire, and the islands of Malta and Gozo as a small enclave within that empire, were beginning to settle down to a routine of colonizer and colonized when the winds of change once more started blowing in the air. As seems to be the destiny of the Mediterranean throughout its history, no sooner has a civilization been established, its language entrenched and its set of beliefs and form of worship firmly anchored than along comes another superpower to upset the balance and supplant all this with a new way of looking at life, at society, at culture, at religion and even at God.

The Maltese Islands, again because of their strategic position at the centre of the Mediterranean could not be left on the sidelines as a new and mighty power took over and spread its influence from Afghanistan in the East to Cadiz in the West and, in a short span of time, conquered all the intervening lands, countries, cultures and civilizations, displacing some, eradicating others, and in general creating havoc all along.

That was the God-given vocation that the charismatic and venturesome Arab Moslem believed he was endowed with, and the rest, as they say, is history.

Chapter 5

The Age of Arab Islam

(From the 8th to the 11th century)

As one super-power in the Mediterranean began to wane another one blossomed to take its place. In its far-flung might, precisely because it had spread itself so far and so wide even unto vulnerable remote areas it could not consolidate or defend, the Byzantine-Hellenic dominance was being challenged by a new and rising power that coupled fierce nomadic warfare strategies with apocalyptic exclusive messianic proselytism.

The religion was Islam and the people were the Arabs.

As such this new power, that combined desert justice with religious liberation swept through much of the Middle and even into parts of the Far East as well as into Europe and North Africa. In fact wherever the Byzantine Empire and the Roman Empire before it had ventured, Islam dared – and gambled further still.

Wherever it went, in keeping with customs of empires of old, it established not only its form of government but also its form of religion. As part of its total package, Islam believed in a theocratic state where the State religion provided the State Law (*shar'ia*). By and large, in those distant days and different times, such super-powers did not have much tolerance for anybody else that stood in their way or anybody that did not agree with their philosophy of life or with their religious view of God and what (they believed) God wanted of the world and the human beings within it.

As we have seen with the Romans and their *Pax Romana*, and with the Goths and Vandals and with the Byzantines, (especially with Constantine making Christianity the favoured religion of his empire), these new conquerors, the Moslems, seldom took any chances in allowing their subjects too much lee-way when it came to freedom of worship or freedom of thought. Besides, within an empire, appointments and promotions went to such of the subjects as embraced the dominant power's set of beliefs – for the obvious reason that, on the face of it, such persons could be better trusted to follow State policies.

It is therefore no surprise that the new empire-builders, the Moslem-Arabs (and eventually the Moslem-Turks allied with them and practising the same Faith) made it obvious that converts to the new Faith, i.e. Islam, would receive preferential treatment: in fact would be relieved of taxes imposed on gentiles (non-believers) and in general would have better chances of promotion and advancement within this theocratic State.

The Arabs must have established in Malta as well that mode of government which was prevalent in the territories that they ruled. And although we do not have any documentation to prove that this was the case, we must presume that Malta was no exception. For under Moslem-Arab rule, a country was ruled by different officials.

There was the *"qa'di"* or *"qa'id"* who handled the day-to-day running of affairs; there was the *"mazalun"* who passed sentences on appeals and such as were outside the competence of the *"qa'di"*. There was the *"Duwana"* for the collection of the *gizja* or taxes and for the keeping of the peace there was the *sahib el-xurta* i.e. the police. Then there was the *"ri'asa"* who mediated between the officials and the community.

In the community, those who had a voice were the heads of the wealthy families, the intellectuals and the heads of the guilds.

We must also presume that, in keeping with the colonial policies of the time, the rulers brooked no opposition. The brutal beheading or cruel exile to a foreign country of the conscientious recalcitrant or the naggingly bothersome opponents of the New Order of Things seemed to be the order of the day whether under Roman, Byzantine or any other mode of government. It also served as a very strong incentive to conversion to the new faith and to an embracing of the conqueror's social as well as political values. It is conceivable that such a method of government under the Moslem-Arabs prevailed in Malta as well. (This rule of law is practised even in this twentieth century in strictly Moslem countries till today; so we are not to think that such practices were not the rule in the pre-Middle Ages. If anything they were more strictly enforced.)

Under the circumstances, in recent years scholars and historians are leaning to the conviction that there was a whole cycle – amounting to hundreds of years – in which the Maltese Islands underwent a profound influence under the Moslem Arabs even to the extent of losing their identity as a Christian nation, with the possibility even that Christianity must have been totally wiped out from Malta or that the Maltese for the major part must have converted to Islam.

To date, for reasons of culture and religion, and mostly because much of the Moslem period of Maltese history was re-written by the Hospitallers and others (whose endemic hatred of anything Moslem led them to the rampant destruction of the traces of the very Moslem presence here), Malta has not been able to come to terms with, still less to acknowledge the fact that a religious cataclysm of this magnitude could have occurred in this Catholic country. This notwithstanding the fact that it was standard *modus operandi* (mode of procedure) in the past: whether the conquerors were pagan Roman, vandalic, or Christians of the Roman Latin or Byzantine Hellenic type.

The religious reasons amount to long-held traditions that the Catholic Faith imparted to Malta by the Apostle Paul (as the Acts of the Apostles loudly proclaim) must have been retained unsullied by the Maltese people from the Year A.D. 60 (the traditional date of

Malta's conversion to the gospel as preached by Paul of Tarsus) right through all the historical vicissitudes that have shaken the islands and on to the present.

All of which includes the unhappy hiatus of the Moslem-Arab presence in Malta.

In spite of it all and through it all, argue those who cannot brook the very idea that Malta lost her Paul-given Christian faith, Malta remained Christian – and more than that, Roman Catholic Apostolic to the core. So, religiously speaking, admitting the possibility of a period, albeit small, when Malta's dominant faith was the Moslem faith would undermine the long-held presumption that Malta has always been Christian of the Roman Catholic and Apostolic kind.

Culturally, Malta finds it difficult to acknowledge that there was an infidel (because non-Christian, and worse non-Catholic) hiatus in its uninterrupted observance of its Christian heritage. Malta has always considered itself part of Europe, Europe has always considered itself a Christian continent and Christianity has always been the sole faith of Europe – with Moorish Spain endured as a temporary historical aberration. Now Malta's European-Christian leanings and links have veered it as far away as possible from a faith called Islam and from a culture called Arabic. As a result, Malta has always considered herself Christian and European – so, at least, does the popular thinking go.

Indeed, Malta, as its historical entanglement with the Hospitallers against the (Turkish) Moslem was to prove later, always acted as the bulwark for Christianity against the infidel – whoever he might be, Turkish-Moslem or Arab-Moslem or Goth or Vandal makes no difference – who has always been considered an invader, an intruder and a heathen!

So for historical researchers even to suggest, as some have done, that there must have been a time, amounting to close to three centuries, when Arab-Moslem influence in Malta was so strong that not only did they rule the islands but that they – as was customary in those days – supplanted the local Christian religion with a foreign Moslem one, and even perhaps went so far as to exterminate the prevalent religion (Christianity) by deporting its local adherents to foreign parts, is a preposterous proposition.

It is more painful still to have to acknowledge such a situation.

As is the fact that it was not outside the parameters of the concept of conquest of the time that an ethnic-cleansing form of revenge (that was quite the norm in the past and is still being practised even in today's so-called civilized world) would be committed by forced rape of the Maltese women and impregnation by the Arab overlords; or failing that, a mass genocide of those who would not accept the new overlords and their new faith and mode of government. These things are happening in our own civilized times, witness the goings-on in ex-Yugoslavia. Imagine in those far-off, might-is-right times when a conqueror had the conquered at his mercy in a ruthless winner-take-all situation.

Familiarity with these sometimes barbaric customs of the late Dark and early Middle Ages will force us also to admit the fact that a conqueror thought nothing of carrying off into slavery the local conquered population – especially one as small as Malta's must have been at the time – and supplanting it with an *imported breed* of people possessing the same cultural and religious sentiments i.e. Arab and Moslem in this particular case. The probability is further compounded by the reflection that as we have seen already, such Arab sympathizers were already present on the islands – brought over as refugees by the Byzantines from Cyrenaica and North Africa.

The acceptance of this very historical possibility – that during the Arab-Moslem reign, Islam was the official religion of Malta – is difficult to accept for many Maltese, even though after all, another Catholic country, Spain has come to terms with and, indeed, survived the acceptance of this Moslem-Arab presence, indeed take-over, in its territory. In fact it has even gained from such a historical encounter and come out the richer for it.

Where would Europe, or indeed the world, be today without the treasures of the literature of Greece (philosophy, science, arts, drama) which only made their way into the western world through Arabic translations preserved by the Arab scholars in Spain? This to take just one example. So in a way, the Moslem-Arab presence in Europe is something to be proud of. For even if we leave aside the passing on of the Greek patrimony that has survived in the Western world due to their preservation in the Arab-Moslem culture, what about the very original contributions of the Arabs themselves: philosophers like Averroes (Ibn-Ruas), Avicenna (Ibn-Sinna) and the rest of the Moslem-Arab intellectuals, the mathematicians, astronomers, historians, poets – all of whom testify to a very advanced civilization and culture?

Be that as it may, Malta has still to go through this catharsis. And this acceptance. It has to acknowledge the facts, which, according to some historians, could have resulted in the complete wiping out of all traces of Christianity from the islands during the sojourn and dominion of the Moslem-Arabs in Malta to be replaced by the Moslem-Arab mode of government, way of thinking, culture and, yes, faith.

Yet to admit all this would amount, to some Maltese, something akin to anathema. An admission made all the more difficult because, in keeping with the accepted winner-takes-all custom when a new conqueror wipes out traces of previous domination, the successive Christian conquerors of Malta (the Normans, Anjevins, Aragonese, Hospitallers) paid them in kind and tried to wipe out all traces of Arab-Moslem presence here.

And so we have very little to go by by way of artifacts, monuments and writings that have survived the successive Christian settlers, and that can throw some light on this important and extensive period of the Arab-Moslem presence in Malta.

However, not all has been irretrievably lost or wiped out.

One sure thing that is indisputably accepted and that cannot be gainsaid is the Moslem-Arab influence on the local language. In fact the Maltese language in vocabulary, structure and syntax is definitely semitic and heavily influenced also by Arabic.

Another pronounced Moslem-Arab influence that has survived in Malta is to be found in the popular way of thinking. This is especially evident in the oriental/islamic fatalistic approach with its well-known resigned approach to destiny – *kismet* – transformed spiritually into *resignation to the inscrutable and non-questionable Will of Allah* for the faithful Moslem, and modified into the *inscrutable and non-questionable Will of Alla* for the Christian Maltese.

It is significant that among the legacies left by a Moslem-Arab world, there is the very word for God: *Allah* in Arabic and *Alla* in Maltese. Among the many other technical religious terms which the Maltese language shares with Moslem-Arabic one can mention: *Għid* (Id – Easter); *randan* (ramadan, lent); *għasar* (vespers); *tewba* (goodness) and, till the end of the fifteenth century the common village celebration currently known as *festa* was called *zerda* – which is the term used at North Africa's Moslem shrines for a similar celebration.

The influence of the Moslem-Arab in Malta extended still further to place-names of which there is quite a number which till today retain their Arab-Moslem origin. To start with the very names of the islands that took their definite appellations from the Arabic: Malta, the Arabic form of Melita; Għawdex rather than Gaulos for Gozo; Kemmuna from the Arab word for the herb cumin (kumin) for Comino; and Filfla from the Arabic felfel.

Besides, there are the names of most of the harbours, as in Marsa itself; the Arabic *marsa* part of Marsa-mxett and Marsa-scala. Others like, Qala, Mġarr, Rabat are of Arab origin as well. But the preponderance that has endured longest is the one in place-names of localities that were furthest removed from succeeding civilizing

Mdina – The silent city – retains much of its old pride when it was the capital city of Malta

influences: Xara (from shari'a – the law of the Koran); Tal-Mislem and Ta' Miselmiet – all place-names with Moslem traces that have survived until today.

But most assuredly, of all the place-names is the name Mdina (Medina) associated with the Moslem-Arab presence in Malta. This was the capital of Malta under and during the time of the Arabs. In typical fashion of the time, it stood on a hill; was defensible because it could be ringed with walls all around and was small enough to contain the total local administrative and surrounding (peasant) population within its bastions in case of a siege.

Arab-Moslem influence is to be found even among Maltese nick-names still in current use today: *Tal-Ħaġ* (one who has made a pilgrimage to Mecca); *Tal-Ġażi* (warrior of Islam); *Ħafis* (one who knew the Koran by heart).

Arab influence can be traced in many family surnames in Malta as well that have survived to this day: Abdilla, Axiaq, Borg, Buhagiar, Buttigieg, Caxaru (Cassar), Fenech, Ebejer, Sammut and a number of others – a sure indication that in spite of trying to wipe out and start with a clean slate under successive Christian sovereigns, some things cannot be wiped out completely.

Another controversy linked to names centres around the name Mohammed which in some form or other (e.g. Ahmed, Mahmood etc.) was a given name or formed part of the name of most males – as it does in the Moslem world till today. During the Arab reign, the name Mohammed as a given name must have been adopted by many Maltese because it is found in name-registers. This led some historians to argue that all Maltese males – and therefore all Maltese – had become Moslem under the Arabs. Except that, after the depature of the Moslems, the custom seems to have fallen into disuse. An argument, hold some, that the adoption of the given name Mohammed during the Moslem-Arab reign must have been motivated by diplomatic and survival reasons rather than religious convictions or conversion.

The Moslems, who bury their dead, left us some indications of their way of life –
in their tombs

The Arab presence in Malta has been also more tangibly asserted by the discovery of tombs especially since the Arabic inscriptions on the stone slabs can give us some sparse though precious information. For one thing they must have had cemeteries, for Moslems, like Christians bury their dead. And secondly even such indications as locations might give us some idea as to where the Moslem population was concentrated. Even such things as dates could provide us with information as to the life-expectancy and such things. Unfortunately there is not much such evidence to go by and on which one can build any theories.

A couple of legacies that are commonly believed to have been left to Malta by the Arabs was the introduction of the cotton seed and hence the promotion of cotton as a major agricultural industry and the introduction of the *sienja* – an animal-driven wheel by which water can be drawn from a well for irrigation purposes. But apart from all this, and a couple of references to the safe havens that are to be found in the islands, there is little historical information to go by relating to this period.

By and large, the effect of the presence of the Arab-Moslem in Malta – which lasted something close to three centuries – evokes strong emotions in Malta, even to this day. There are those who, in the mode of liberal thinkers and more specifically as defenders of the universal freedom of religion would have no difficulty admitting even a complete take-over by the Arabs of the Maltese islands in such a way that for that period of time even Malta's national religion was Islam. On the other hand there are those who, harping on the European roots and faith of the Maltese nation, would brook no such hiatus. They might concede that the lower echelons of Maltese society – who do not make much difference anyhow to the general outcome – along with some imported riff-raff might have practised this foreign faith. But not the Maltese that counted, which in this case were the upper classes, and as we shall see from now on – with the noble houses of the Normans and of Anjou, as well as the Monarchy of Aragon

Malta today boasts of a modern mosque in Paola

and the aristocratic Hospitallers – meant nearly only and always, the nobility, the elite of Malta.

However, right now through the Kingdoms, big and small, of Europe a new challenge was being faced and a new gospel was being preached: the Crusades. The various Kingdoms of that continent called Europe were going through tremendous upheavals as the first wafts of the spirit of the crusades raised the hue and the cry to free the Land called Holy from the control of Islam. This same crusading spirit unleashed the spirit of adventure and conquest and chivalry and legend that was to animate a number of European nations to fight against and conquer others, especially those that were controlled by the infidels: the Moslem-Arabs. In most cases the religious motivation – to return these Moslem-dominated nations back to Christianity – was as far removed from the actual intentions as could be. Be that as it may, Malta lay in the path of a new conquering nation, that happened to be Christian and that happened to come from the North – the Normans. And the Normans paid more than a courtesy visit here.

Chapter 6

The Age of
Ruthless Norman Coarseness

(1091, 1127 and all that – till 1266)

Count Roger has for a long time been considered by many Maltese as the one who saved Malta from the domination of the supposedly much-hated Arab-Moslem despots during whose reign, for close to three centuries, the local Christians – or whatever remnant of them was left on the islands, if any – had been suffering religious persecution for their Christian faith. But holding on to one's faith will bring its own rewards in the form of a saviour who will deliver the oppressed people form their exploiters.

And this happened, eventually, in that fateful year of 1091.

The Maltese, oppressed under the Moslem rule, were visited for the first time by this *Northman* called Count Roger who liberated them and negotiated for the natives the freedom to practise their true and original Christian faith as it had been passed on to them and preached on the islands by Paul back in the Year A.D. 60 – or at least in that form in which it had survived coloured as it had become by Byzantine and other influences.

As he entered the Gates of Mdina in triumph and to the acclamation of the beleaguered populace to take possession of the Maltese Islands, Count Roger, hailing all the way from Normandy, was so moved by the swelling crowds greeting him that he tore a

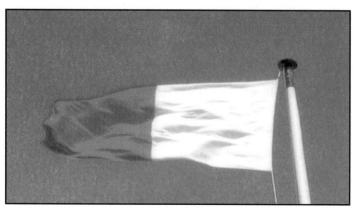

The Maltese flag – red and white squares – is traditionally believed to go back to Roger's time

section of his chequered white-and-red flag and gave it to the Maltese – and ever since then Malta has had its national red-and-white flag. At least, so goes a popular legend in Malta. But do not try to tell the local believers in such legends that the practice for conquering armies to carry distinctive banners came much later in history. And hence the legend of the Rogerian origin of the Maltese flag is simply that, a legend.

So much for the legends that very often go for historical fact even though much of the above is narrated as gospel-truth. In fact, it has been traditional historical fare for years in Malta and only recently is all this being questioned by serious historians.

If one asks how such legends could become accepted historical facts, one would find that it is all probably due to the non-critical acceptance by Maltese historians in the past of material that was at most a wishful re-writing of history to suit the local particular religious slant. This becomes more plausible still when one considers that the earlier historians were all Catholics and clerics to boot and they held a monopoly over research material as well as access to same. That such reading of history often did violence to historical investigation and objective truth bothered not too many people at all as long as the devout interpretation of history expected to lean heavily towards the Catholic way was safeguarded.

Today, with more non-clerical, lay people in the historical field and with the opening up of archives hitherto inaccessible to the public, a more objective assessment of historical facts is possible from independent and sometimes non-Church scholars and sources – which is why certain pet theories, including the origins of the Maltese flag as a gift from Count Roger are being rejected as not corresponding to historical fact.

The truth – as it is being unearthed by contemporary serious historians – would show a somewhat different version of what actually happened.

A word about the Normans

The Normans hailed from that powerful Kingdom called Normandy. The Normans were settlers, Northmen – Vikings and Danes – who had come from the Scandinavian countries, settled in that part of the Atlantic coast (which is now the north-west province of modern France), converted to Christianity, had taken on civilized customs and set about consolidating their power and spreading their Northman ambitions by conquering the rest of Europe.

Their holy intentions received further papal approval in 1059 at the regional synod of Melfi when Pope Nicholas II legitimized the hitherto anarchic Normans into a respectable force. Empowered and blessed by the Roman Church to oust the Byzantine schismatics and the Moslem Arabs from the rest of Europe, they took this as *carte blanche* to build the Norman Empire – which meant pushing their conquering drive to the southern regions of Europe as well – which is how Malta was affected.

In the 11th century we find Tancred's descendents of the Hauteville family encroaching beyond Rome and further south. They took Benevento, Salerno and Capua from the Longobards; went to Abruzzi, Puglia, Basilicata and Calabria and took them from the Byzantines; took over Amalfi, Naples and Sorrento even though these were independent dukedoms; and proceeded on to Moslem Sicily and *its islands* – which is what the Maltese archipelago was considered: the islands-appendage of Sicily, and which is how the Normans ended up with Count Roger in Malta.

Count Roger had settled the score with the Moslems in Sicily and then proceeded on to Malta. Sensing that with a superior force he could easily overcome the peaceful lords and masters who at that time lived in Medina, the then capital of Malta, Count Roger figured that it would not hurt his sovereign's expansionist plans – once he had come all the way to Sicily – to claim this blob of land in the name of his Norman King. After all, Malta was an important stop-over place in the shipment of supplies as well as a safe refuge during storms, and as such a trophy to be prized.

Taking stock of a situation and considering that, if the worst came to the worst, the closest Moslem ally that could send help to a besieged Malta was 120 miles to the south in North Africa, he figured he could take some risks for this peach of a place to fall in his lap. To test the enemy's strength, he harried the country-side for a couple of days or so, and this show of force must have decided matters.

The representative (Moslem) government at Mdina promised to recognize Roger as the sovereign of Malta and Gozo, agreed to pay an annual tribute – as was customary – in recognition of this sovereignty and to surrender their Christian captives. The Norman side swore to the pact using the Bible or the Cross; while the Maltese side swore to the same pact on the Koran.

And so a new era, for Malta, was launched.

The Normans in Malta

However, the era was not launched by the total and wholesale substitution of one regime by another when Count Roger visited here in 1091. There was no immediate *normanization* of Malta. Until such time as they could be substituted, the Arab-Moslems who had been governing Malta could remain in control. For a time, it seems in fact till much later (more like a century), the Moslem presence in Malta continued to dominate as can be seen from the fact that they continued to bury their dead here in tombs that are to be found in the islands (even as there were no contemporary Christian tombs – at least none that have to date been found).

In fact there is reason to believe that the Norman Conquest of Malta in 1091 was not a permanent one for the Normans had to re-visit Malta in 1127 under Count Roger II – when they came to stay. This was dictated partly by the turn events had taken in Christendom – the Crusades – which were out-and-out warfare of Christians against Moslems. It also meant that taking over complete control from the *infidels* became a Christian imperative.

In their wake and after their first visit, the Normans must have left a skeleton administrative delegation to run and to rule; a garrison of military personnel to help keep law and order by force where persuasion failed, and a number of clerics of the Latin as well as the Greek rites to cater to these Christians left behind, as well as to instruct the converts to the (Christian) Faith.

As time went on, the slow substitution of one form of government with another and one national religion with another took place – sometimes violently as often happened in those far-away times, but more probably rather slowly because the Normans were a tolerant people and they allowed the locals to worship as they pleased and practise their faith without hindrance.

The local colonial government

All in all, the Normans are known to have adopted a tolerant attitude wherever they went by respecting the local form of government and not imposing their own – a clever political and diplomatic ploy dictated by circumstances, seeing that their homeland was so far away and defending impositions and local insurrections so difficult to effect. This is why perhaps, historians believe that the Arab-Moslem method of governing prevailing on the island must have been respected and only once they were fully and completely entrenched did the Normans take over.

The form of local government under the Normans saw the setting up of a Captain of the Harbour who had an important role especially since the Normans were on friendly terms with Pisa, Venice and Genoa whose fleets, roaming the Mediterranean, were a force to be reckoned with. On the islands, there must have been a Captain of the Courts. The *Baiulaccio* saw to the collection of taxes especially such as related to customs duties. There must also have been a Health Officer to look after the health of the populace and enforce the quarantines as necessary. There must have been as well another official representing the King in his domains who would see to the proper distribution of 'royal' land and collection of taxes therefrom.

The re-establishment of Christianity as the national faith

Of primary importance, because of common European concern, was the re-establishment of the Christian faith as the national faith. Christians who must have gone underground or, as peasants, lived away from centres of authority under the Moslem reign, now came out of the woodwork. Others who had become *Moslems of convenience* re-converted back to Christianity – probably now becoming *Christians of convenience*. (It would not be stretching the imagination too much to believe that the same thing happened here as happened in Spain with the *Maranos* – the Jews who, because of the religious

Mdina still retains vestiges of its Norman past

persecutions, pretended to convert to Christianity while deep down they retained their Jewish identity and faith. The Christians could have converted to Islam out of convenience, only to re-convert back to Christianity to accommodate the new rulers who were Christians).

Once the new Norman overlords decided to settle permanently in Malta and came here to stay – which apparently they did in 1171, they took steps to establish themselves in such a way as to make sure that the Christian faith would be entrenched here as well. Being *westerners* they of course favoured and promoted the Latin and not the Byzantine (Oriental) rite in their worship. In fact, as was customary with the Crusades already, they must have carried with them their own chaplains, the clergy from their own Normandy, to minister to them. The Normans, therefore, soon established themselves as overlords in Malta – thus becoming a self-contained elite enclave in this foreign outpost.

As did their western, Latin rite in their form of worship.

However, one can find in Malta Byzantinesque style of wall-paintings dating to these post-Islamic Norman times which can only be explained by the fact that the Greek rite was tolerated on the islands. This can be explained by the presence of the Christian immigrants that came from Sicily and perhaps Southern Italy and who were accompanied by Basilian monks and hermits of the Oriental rite – who, in turn, ministered to them.

It is thus probable that the Greek rite, typically, was relegated to an inferior status: to the immigrant and lower class communities. (This merely indulgent toleration of the Greek rite on the part of the Latins was part and parcel of the politics/philosophy of the time – and for centuries to come: even though both Greeks and Latins were equally Christian and equally apostolic, the Latins viewed the Greeks with something less than brotherly acceptance and the two modes of worship in the same Christian faith did not always enjoy equal status or even mutual acceptance.)

So it is quite consonant with contemporary thinking that such an attitude prevailed in Malta as well. In fact, as time went on and, a generation or so later, a number of the indigenous Moslem inhabitants in Malta thought it expedient to convert to Christianity, these converts opted for the Greek rather than the Latin rite – thereby further, perhaps, increasing the social gap that existed between Latin rite conquerors and subject Greek rite faithful and converts.

The enthusiastic chorus with which Count Roger and his Normans are believed to have been hailed as the saviours of Christianity in Malta has to be mitigated again by another consideration. As we have seen the ruling (Norman) classes visibly belonged to the Establishment Church that observed the Latin rite which in turn catered to their spiritual and other needs. The subject peoples – and Moslem converts – embraced the Greek rite, visibly an inferior rite in the eyes of the overlords. The Latin rite, as the mode of worship of the conquerors, was likened to the Establishment Church while the Oriental Greek rite was considered inferior because it was observed by the common people and converts. One can imagine that the overlords could afford to feel superior because the financial support of the Establishment Church came from abroad and not from the local faithful.

To start with, the bishop at this time (first mentioned in 1153) – and for centuries later – resided in Sicily. In a practice that was to merit the censure of the Fathers gathered at the Council of Trent in the 16th century, absentee bishops were the rule rather than the exception, and Malta, in this matter, was no exception.

The bishopric was a fiefdom-honour bestowed on noble dignitaries and in the feudal system of the time, it was endowed with extensive benefices in the shape of revenue-yielding estates. So the Bishop did not have to depend for his sustenance on the presence of any Christians in his particular diocese at all – which was no spur to make him seek to enlarge his flock by seeking converts.

Eventually the Latin rite (probably seen in the perception of

Norman-inspired architecture at Mdina

the populace as the more affluent and therefore more powerfully convincing) took over as the majority rite even as Islam was, by the decree of 1249 suppressed in these islands and its last open adherents exiled to Lucera (in Central Italy).

The Norman Legacy

Much as the imagination of the local population has been fired by the later writers of history about the crucial role of the Normans in re-establishing the Christian faith as the one and only true faith for these islands after the Moslem hiatus, a less passionate and more objective assessment must conclude that much of what the Normans did, like all that conquering nations before them and since have done, centred around consolidating their dominion in the conquered lands. Even though, as we have seen, these particular conquerors were rather tolerant – for practical and diplomatic reasons more than religious ones. The conquerors did not mix with the conquered and there is no reason to believe that in a medieval pyramidal society, the Normans ever mixed with the local people. They used the local power-structure, again in the hands of the powerful families, to re-inforce and bolster their own sovereignty. If the local Christian community was split into two by the two different forms of worship, Roman Latin and Oriental Greek, so be it. The superior rite of the conquerors as the Established Church would stand out all the more and re-inforce the social chasm that existed between conquerors and conquered.

This is an important historical element because it set the stamp for Malta's eventual leaning to the Roman-Latin type of Christianity with its very tiered and hierarchical structure that went well with a fiefdom mentality.

Politically, the Maltese islands were an island-colony of Normandy; they were never anywhere close to self-government. Rather one must say that with the imposition of the *rulers from abroad and above*, the mentality began to be ingrained pretty early that the

Maltese needed others to rule them, to guide them, to administer their islands for they were incapable of doing it themselves.

Matters did not improve, either, when Count Roger II established the Kingdom of the Two Sicilies in 1139. Now Malta's fate began to be linked more closely with that of Sicily and Naples, to be dwarfed still further by these two big neighbours. Matters did not improve either, under the House of Anjou or the Kingdom of Aragon – the next two big powers to occupy Malta before the arrival of the Knights Hospitallers of St John of Jerusalem – as we shall have occasion to see.

Chapter 7

The Age of Anjevin Brutality

(1266 – 1283)

If one could unravel a very dark and complicated period in European history when, actually, there was no Europe as such but a disparate number of fiefdoms with noble, and not so noble, families each fighting the other to annex new territory, or marrying off into another dynasty to consolidate its territorial claims then perhaps one can begin to understand the period of history with which we have to deal next.

Fiefdoms were fought over, fought for, used as bargaining chips and disposed of for the right price – with the subjects within these fiefdoms having little say in the matter. During this period, vicious partisans like Ghibellines (pro German-emperor sympathizers) and Guelphs (pro-papacy supporters) fought each other in the name of Christianity at a time when the Pope in Rome was very much a military leader with his own papal states and, as Head of the Holy Roman Empire, spent more of his time and energy in the administration of material matters than in the strictly spiritual governance of Christianity.

At this time, too, the crusading idea of liberating the Holy Land from the control of the infidel, Turk or otherwise made no difference, had achieved greater urgency. However this supposedly Christian vocation took second place on the part of some kings and nobles to the chivalric sense of adventure and slaughtering of the enemy just for the sake of it. It was therefore no surprise that treason, betrayal, poisonings, hypocrisy and murder were the order of the day and since very often the normal administration of justice was non-existent since it devolved around those with the strongest armies and the strongest forces, might became right. The concept of baronial conspiracies germinated – that was to set the stage for what later was to develop into the *omertà* type of justice that came to be popularly known as *mafia*.

Within such a framework it is also understandable that piracy on the high seas – which at this time was limited mostly to the Mediterranean Sea – took the shape of a lucrative business tempting many into the lure of quick spoils. And in this, private fleets and the adventurous men to equip them created a new mode of existence and a new source of revenue.

If one can understand all this, then perhaps one can begin to penetrate the complicated mess that is the Middle Ages. And the brutal mentality that prevailed during this turbulent period in Europe.

First of all the idea of fiefdoms where valued pieces of property – sometimes whole nations and islands, or groups of islands as in the case of the Maltese archipelago – were deeded to some nobleman or other, oftentimes as absentee landlords, was very common practice. That these then went ahead and exacted all sorts of benefits for themselves in the shape of cash and kind in taxes and produce merely for allowing some poor and destitute vassals the privilege of working the landlord's domain was also a common way of doing business.

The Guelphs and the Ghibellines were ideologies, two great parties whose conflicts made so much of the history of Italy and Germany in the 12th, 13th and 14th centuries. In Italy, the Guelphs (the Italian adaptation of the original *Welfe*, the family name and battle-cry of Henry the Lion, Duke of Bavaria) embraced the anti-imperialistic therefore popular parties that happened to be also pro-pope. Then there were such nation-states as Venice and Genoa that threw in their support with this party.

The Ghibellines on the other hand, who got their name from the corruption of *Waiblingen* (the battle cry used by the Hohenstaufen Emperor Conrad III, Duke of Franconia at the battle of Weinsberg in 1140) were the pro-German sympathizers in Italy. Florence was among such states with sympathies leaning towards German imperialism.

In the defence and sustenance of the Holy Roman Empire, the setting up of which is considered by some historians as one of the biggest judgmental errors on the part of the papacy's long history, papal influence and arm-twisting often tilted the balance of power among the feudal states. Such papal interference extended to prodding kings to send soldiers to fight in foreign territories as happened to the saintly Louis IX of France whose soldiers were sent to that (anti-popish) island called Sicily. The king's brother Charles of Anjou had received the Kingdom of the Two Sicilies (Naples and Sicily) from Pope Urban IV in 1266. But to claim it, Charles had had to defeat the Hohenstaufen Manfred, son of Frederic II.

The Pope had gone ahead and crowned Charles King of Sicily on the 6th of January 1266: which is how Malta, being allied so closely to Sicily, in fact being often seen as nothing much more than a fiefdom appendage of Sicily, passed under the Anjevins. Not that Malta was not lucky in that at least it was geographically far enough from Sicily to receive its doses of Anjevin cruelty by delayed mandates. For the Anjevin rule was harsh and cruel and the Anjevins soon managed to make themselves hated by the Sicilians who had no form of redress other than periodic forms of vengeful sabotage with the consequent cohesive bond of solidarity and the pledge of silence among the perpetrators.

The form of government under the Anjevins

As to Malta and the Maltese, there is reason to believe that under the Anjevins the Maltese archipelago retained the same form of government as it had had previously. It was now ruled by a Governor, the king's lieutenant who was at one and the same time the administrator as well as the commandant and overseer of the defences. His job was to see to the total and overall administration of the islands that included the collection of taxes for his king, as well as seeing to the construction and repairs of the defences of the islands to safeguard them from the marauding corsairs that roamed the Mediterranean.

Eventually, probably because this was too much for one man or perhaps because some other nobleman ambitioned to the possibility of sharing some of the spoils, the duties were split up and different people were assigned to different roles. Thus, there comes a time in 1271 when Charles I of Anjou decreed that his representative in Malta would retain the duty of Castellan while the other duties, like Administrator, Procurator and Commander would be distributed among other gentlemen.

One such worthy was a Maltese by the name of Robert Kaforio who in 1273 was appointed Master and Treasurer of the Maltese Islands to thus ease the Administrator's burden in his heavy duties of running the islands. Kaforio was also assigned the responsibility of taking an inventory of those goods that might be of interest to the Imperial Court. The king meant this duty to be taken seriously, so much so that he dispatched a couple of gentlemen, Matthew de Podio and Peter de Argellerio to help in expediting matters.

As is to be expected when your overseers are so far away, the temptation to abuse one's power and trust are too great to be resisted by mere mortals and this Maltese functionary was very much a mere mortal. He did not fulfill his duties to the complete satisfaction of the Crown (actually he was accused of embezzlement) and he was removed from office, with his erstwhile assistant, Matthew de Podio now willingly filling in and taking up the duties of Castellan himself.

Under the Anjevins, Malta remained also the breeding ground

for falcons and leopards – a trend that had been started under the Normans. As to the falcons, they may have abounded in Malta partly because at that time the migratory route of various birds must have taken them through Malta, for there must definitely have been more wilderness at the time and more watering-holes as well: so the falcons had plenty of prey to feed on. As to the leopards, these must definitely have been raised in captivity.

The Uprising – the 'Vespri Siciliani'

As is to be expected in a time when one maritime or military power or other is always jostling for position and trying to oust the other, the Anjevins were soon being challenged by the Aragonese for the control of the Mediterranean. This outside pressure was further abetted by the deep state of discontent within the Anjevin Kingdom, two factors that contributed to an inevitable denouement which happened with the famous *Vespri Siciliani* – an event that was to be immortalized in the famous operatic work of the same name.

It went something like this: the state of Naples which, as part of the Kingdom of the Two Sicilies, was also under the Anjevins harboured a man named John in one of its islands called Prochyta. He was a disgruntled personage who wanted to get rid of the Anjevin yoke and hence became an Aragonese sympathizer. This gentleman planned to destroy them completely with the help of the Genoans and the Venetians – the eternal enemies of the Anjevins. John of Prochyta went to Constantinople to collect funds and sympathy and thence on to Trapani (in Sicily) to make the final plans. But on learning that the Pope (Nicholas) had died, he ordered the conspirators to proceed clandestinely to Malta where the final and perhaps alternative plans would be drawn up.

The conspiracy against the French (which was hatched in Malta) came to be known as *I Vespri Siciliani*, The Sicilian Vespers because the uprising and massacre began at the time of Vespers (the evening Church service) of Easter Tuesday of the year 1282. It was a brutal and bloody massacre where the casualties on both sides were very great but where pent-up hatred on the part of the Sicilians blinded them to the limits to which vengeance and anger could go.

Thus the Sicilians were finally rid of Charles and the dynastic ambitions of the Anjevins in their island. These latter had ruled them with an iron hand and had been very harsh masters indeed. In fact, the Anjevins during their occupation in Sicily were generally hated – and there is no reason to suspect that they were not hated in Malta as well, or that their mode of government was any different here.

Within a month of this fateful Easter Tuesday, all the Anjevins had to flee from Sicily and the crown was later given to Pedro III of Aragon. But even then his rule was not free of plots and conspiracies and many a time during his reign did he have to thwart Anjevin attempts at re-occupation. Pedro passed the crown to his son who came to be known as Frederic III of Sicily.

The Anjevins in Malta

Whatever can be said about Anjevin rule in Sicily can be said for Malta for there is no reason to believe that the form of government was any less harsh or any less brutal, and there is no reason to suspect that they were any the less hated in Malta. But the ousting of the Anjevins from Sicily did not mean the end of their brutal reign here. Unfortunately for Malta, this was one time in history when the course followed in these islands did not parallel the events happening in Sicily. Here, the Anjevins re-inforced their positions and entrenched themselves still further – for a time. For eventually the Aragonese fleet paid a visit to Malta as well – if nothing else to test the waters.

In fact, in July 1283, in a battle that took place in the harbour of Malta, the Aragonese fleet routed the Anjevin fleet and brought an end to the Anjevin dynasty in Malta as well. Thus the Anjevins were unseated from Sicily – and Malta.

However they still retained their hold on Naples!

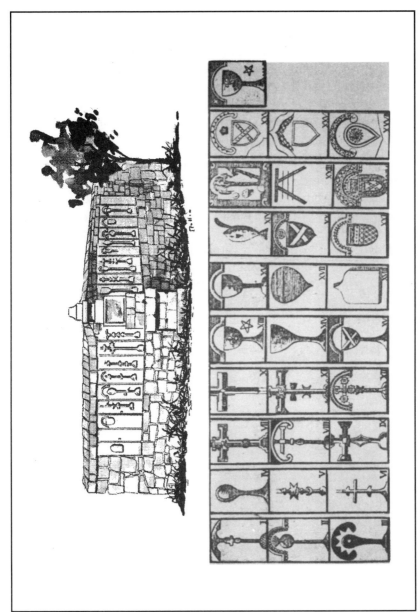

The cemetery in Rabat (Gozo) where "Crusader remains" were found

Did the Anjevin rule leave any legacies or remarkable reminders in the islands? Apparently none that have survived bar some human bones from a cemetery in Rabat (Gozo). As the record left us by the Bishop of Malta, Paul de Alpheran centuries later (1755) tells us, the Bishop collected the *holy remains of bishops and well-known persons who had accompanied Louis, King of France in the holy war in Africa and of the Frenchmen who ruled the island [of Gozo] and laid them to rest all together in this holy place [cemetery]*.

In this he must have been moved by respect for the dead as well as admiration for fellow-clerics and Frenchmen and a desire to have their deeds remembered by posterity. After all the king referred here was Louis IX of France who was known as the *Pious* and in fact was to be canonized as a saint. We know that he participated in two crusades in Africa – one (the seventh crusade) to Egypt and another one (the eighth crusade) to Tunis, where he met his death. It is intriguing to speculate whether the bones of the saintly king as well as those of the fellow-crusaders who died with him in Tunis might have been transferred to Malta to be laid to rest in some cemetery in Rabat, Gozo!

All in all, though, the Maltese just like the Sicilians were glad to be rid of the Anjevins whose reign, though short, was remembered with hatred as one of horror. The only fly in the ointment is that their successors, the Aragonese, were not much better.

Chapter 8

The Age of Aragonese Treachery

(1283–1530)

As often happens in history, no sooner does one power begin to wane than another rises on the horizon. In fact, the Anjevin supremacy of the Mediterranean had been consistently challenged for some time now by the new shining star in the Mediterranean, the Kingdom of Aragon. This was made up of those provinces of northern Spain known as the Crown of Aragon that included Aragon, Catalonia and Valencia. In the end, after all the skirmishes and the pin-pricks, there came a time when Aragonese supremacy superseded the House of Anjou and thus took control of most of the states in Europe which, as we know, at the time was not united into one cohesive continent but was merely a conglomeration of City-states which happened to be on a single geographical piece of land, constantly fighting each other. In truth, the animosity that pervaded each dynasty and each provincial allegiance makes historians wonder how Europe ever came to be united at all.

In the late thirteenth century, King Peter III ruled as the King of Aragon and with the conquest of Sicily he had become now also king of that island as well as of its ancillary islands. In this part of the Mediterranean he was known as Peter I of Sicily. With his expansionist policies of conquering whatever could be conquered in the then known world, the Mediterranean, His Majesty was not loathe to add the Maltese Archipelago to his southern Mediterranean possessions. In fact, he was so sure that Malta would capitulate and come to the Aragonese fold that the official document of Malta's accession was signed on the 9th June 1283, well before – a full five months – his admiral Roger de Lauria took over control of that blob of land in Malta known as *Castellimar* (Borgo) but which was the seat of local power.

For at the time this strategic entrance to the harbour along with the capital city Medina were basically what constituted the seat of government of these islands. And, in the mentality of the feudal times, once the seat of government was occupied, the rest of the country had little chance of preventing total and absolute surrender to or domination by the conquerors.

The fact that the Maltese by and large had spent a period of disillusionment and bitterness as a result of the harshness and brutality of the Anjevin reign in the Maltese archipelago may have had something to do with this readiness on the part of the local populace to accede to the demands of this new Mediterranean naval power. The fact that the Maltese could not offer any meaningful or weighty resistance was, sensibly, another reason.

Still and all, one cannot say that the Aragonese were welcomed with open arms in Malta. As often happens, there were those among the local population, especially such as had benefited from association with the previous masters, who cherished nostalgic ties with the Anjevins now that they found themselves out of favour with the present ones.

These pockets of unrest were to result in periodic flare-ups that took place here. In fact, even after their departure from Malta, the seeds of such discontent were sown and nurtured by the Anjevins from their stronghold, the Kingdom of Naples – which had remained loyal to the House of Anjou and which was close enough strategically to cause the Aragonese in Sicily and Malta a lot of harassment if not harm. The Anjevins even went to the extent of placing their fleet outside the Maltese harbour to serve as an incentive to any among the discontented members of the local population.

However, the Aragonese would tolerate no such temptations. The house of Aragon under Peter set itself on an expansionist course, so much so that it was to earn Peter the nickname *the Great*. He set about making vassals loyal to Aragon of as many of the Mediterranean countries as possible. To achieve this, he realized that the maritime supremacy of Aragon had to be nourished, strengthened, asserted and acknowledged beyond question. This meant, in turn, that the Anjevin power, along with that of their partners, the sea-faring Genoese and Venetians, had to be annihilated.

Once such undoubted supremacy was established, one could negotiate from a position of strength. Not that a word, even one solemnly given and earnestly pledged meant that it could not be broken! And this mode of treacherous goings-on, perhaps more than anything else, characterizes this Aragonese period as an age of tyranny or as some have more mildly put it, the age of feudal anarchy.

Aragon Treachery at its best

The first taste the Maltese had of such treachery came soon enough – with the very sons of Peter III himself: Alfons, James and Frederic.

Peter had divided his empire between his two elder sons, Alfons and James. Alfons became King of Aragon while James became King of Sicily. The latter had promised the Sicilians he would be their king forever and never leave them. He had also solemnly promised that, should the worst come to the worst, he would keep Sicily within the Aragonese empire. However, five years later, on the death of his brother Alfons, James became King of Aragon with the title of James II.

In Aragon, times had changed from the days when (father) Peter was king. So much so that now the new Aragonese king, James, was already bargaining with the Pope (Boniface VIII, in 1295) to cede Sicily and its islands (i.e. the Maltese archipelago and Pantelleria) in exchange for Sardinia and Corsica. Probably he saw that it made more sense to incorporate these two big islands into his Kingdom rather than Sicily and the small fry attached to it. After all Sardinia and Corsica, being closer to Aragon, were strategically more easily defensible than those far-away islands like Sicily and Malta and Pantelleria.

Forget about promises made to the Sicilians (and hence even to Malta) when he had been their king that they would forever remain part of the Aragonese empire. But chalk one up for royal treachery – one in a never-ending series that was to see the Sicilian Kingdom (along, very often, with the Maltese archipelago and Pantelleria – which were considered as one entity and whose fate therefore was linked with that of its bigger sister-island) bartered back and forth and sometimes sold outright like pieces of very disposable real estate.

Be that as it may, when the Sicilians got wind of this betrayal on the part of James, they shifted their allegiance and chose as their king, James II's younger brother, Frederic, who was Peter's third son. They proclaimed him their king as Frederic III in Catania in January 1296 – a title and Kingdom he was to keep for the 41 years of his long reign.

To show that he meant business and especially that he meant to be loyal to Sicily, King Frederic published the *Constitutio Fredericiana* in which he basically swore fidelity to the Sicilians and pledged never to desert the islands or barter them or give in to diplomatic arrangements, even if the corresponding negotiator were none other than the pope himself. Frederic III, king of Sicily, meant to endear himself to the Sicilians and be their faithful king.

All of this, of course, displeased both his brother, James II King of Aragon as well as the Pope, head of all Christendom. The former sent a punitive fleet to wreak havoc on Pantelleria, Malta and Gozo where they burned and plundered and ravaged to their hearts' content, while the Pope punished the Maltese for their allegiance to Frederic and disloyalty to James II by not appointing a bishop when the local see became vacant.

The royal perfidy that Sicily – and hence Malta – were made to undergo set the tone of the long Aragonese dynasty that became the *modus operandi* and was to stamp these Mediterranean islands for many years to come: kings, monarchs and noblemen did not think twice of breaking their word or their pledge, no matter how solemnly given. And with this royal example of treachery to go by, the subjects felt that they could pay royalty – and each other – back in kind.

Thus we have a long reign, with a feudal system based on bartering and selling off to the highest bidder or to the best proponent. All of which necessarily brought about a lack of overall trust and credibility.

Following a set pattern

After that first betrayal of Sicily by King James II, a chain of others was to follow.

Some of the baser ones.

In Sicily, King Frederic III soon had his hands full trying to keep the local barons in line and preventing them from conspiring against him to overthrow him. To offset this, Frederic III appointed his son, Peter II as his lieutenant who set about re-arranging things which included, among others, that of donating fiefdoms to his noblemen-vassals. Among these donations to noblemen were the islands of Malta and Gozo.

Another occasion, another donation: this time of the Maltese islands as a dowry! When Frederic III gave his daughter Doña

Lucina in marriage to Moncada, he promised her Malta and Gozo for her dowry until someone, so the story goes, whispered into the royal ear that the islands were a jewel to be prized and not pieces of real estate to be given away lightly especially to a son-in-law who may turn out not to be fully appreciative of such royal largesse! Moncada received the City of Augusta instead of Malta and Gozo.

As the thirteenth century gave way to the fourteenth, in 1300 the islands of Malta and Gozo passed into the hands of Roger de Flor, a German of *noble* descent who after leaving the Templar Order under doubtful circumstances, took to piracy on the high seas. Eventually he too got tired of this gem of an island and from Roger de Flor, Malta passed into the hands of Don Juan, the other son of Frederic III who now became the new viceroy.

Even when Don Juan succeeded his father and became king, history repeated itself with regrettable monotony and even this king, who had decreed in 1350 that Malta was placed under the direct protection of the king in a privilege known as *Regio Demanio*, went ahead and feuded Malta to his lieutenant in Messina, Angelo Cazzolio in 1352!

A few years later when the Anjevin Queen of Naples, Juana I captured Messina from the Aragonese, the fate of Malta which had become linked to that city because they were owned by the same Angelo Cazzolio, now passed into Anjevin hands again for the Queen donated the islands to Nicol de Aezerolis who was given the title of Duke of Malta. He passed the title and the fiefdom to his son Angel who in turn passed it on to his own son Robert. However, in 1369 the islands reverted back to the Aragonese – this time in the person of Manfredi Chiaramonte.

This ping-pong mode of government and fluctuating demands on their loyalty displeased the Maltese no end especially when, after a particularly heavy attack on Malta by pirates was repulsed, Frederic IV King of Aragon visited the islands in 1372. The local subjects renewed their loyalty to the king and expected words of encouragement and signs of acknowledgement of their loyalty in return.

The king however was more keen on removing Anjevin influence from the Mediterranean by buying off the Kingdom of Naples from the Anjevins. But to do this he needed gold and silver – and lots of these precious metals. By promising the Maltese during his visit here increased prosperity because of increased trade with the Kingdom of Naples if it ever became part of the Aragonese Empire, he conned the Maltese nobility into donating their gold and silver for the cause. They willingly succumbed to this royal temptation in the hope that this would be an investment in future preferential treatment.

No need to say that little of the promised prosperity ever materialized especially since a few years later (1377) Frederic IV died and nothing but anarchy ruled in his Kingdom.

This state of anarchy was particularly rife in the nearby King-dom of Sicily where plots and counter-plots, conspiracies and acts of vengeance saw this island, by 1396, split up into four *vicariates* – with the Maltese Islands arbitrarily, but fatefully forming part of the Chiaramonte vicariate which included Palermo, Girgenti, Trapani, Val di Noto and Modica.

Thus, all the vicissitudes battering this vicariate were now automatically part and parcel of the lot of the Maltese as well: the islands were straightaway donated to William Raymond of Moncada, Count of Augusta.

Towards the end of the century, with Martin known as the Elder on the throne of Aragon, we have new taxes for Malta amounting to 5% of the income accruing to the islands from piracy, even as Malta was to subsidize and maintain its own fleet and make a collection for the royal wedding of his son Martin (known as the Younger) to Bianca of Navarre. A certain Ingeraldu Inguanez is sent to Malta to make sure that the Maltese do not forget that dues have to be exacted.

The beginning of the fifteenth century sees Martin the Younger on the throne and under him Malta did not receive any better treatment. Nor under the widowed Queen Bianca who took over the reins of government when her husband died. Nor when this latter re-married the son of King Ferdinard, Juan Duke of Piñafel who now became the Viceroy of Sicily and its dependencies. The taxes and the feudal high-handedness go on unabated. Not only that but to all this is now added the methodical attacks from corsairs based in Tunis and other North African ports with the consequent ravages to country-side and decimation of population (carried away to slavery) that such unwelcome assaults brought in their wake.

In fact this pattern was repeatedly in vogue, in spite of royal assurances of protection and vassal (misplaced as it turned out) presumption of fidelity to royal word. And so life went on its perfidious way with never a king or nobleman keeping his word.

But enough about the petty and not so petty perfidy, treachery and deceit among the royal personages and of these towards their vassals. Let us turn to an analysis of the times and try to conjure up life in the feudal system as it prevailed in Malta.

The common every day life in Malta

What about the common and not so common everyday life of the people in Malta?

1. The mode of government

No matter who reigned over Malta and where such feudal king, queen or duke had his residence, it behoved them to keep the local governmental infrastructure in place. After all, in a strictly pyramidal, despotic and autocratic form of government, the local *elders* were the ones who were taxed by the absentee feudal landlords and who therefore had to collect enough taxes to pay the foreigner as well as to collect dues from such liaison-service for themselves.

Hence, we have reason to believe that the Aragonese honoured the system of government prevailing in the islands and retained it as and when it suited them. Even though there is no reason to believe that they had any qualms about replacing or deposing underlings as and when their feudal interests demanded such measures.

Locally, it seems, there were two governing bodies.

The first was the parliamentary assembly or *Commune* (known under various names as *parlamentu generali, consiglio popolare*). The second was the Consiglio Particolare (or università).

The first, the Commune, was made up of the influential people in the islands along with the mayors and representatives of each parish or village who were chosen each year, on the Feast of St John the Baptist (24th June), from among those in the 18 to 60-year bracket. This assembly used to be convoked at the peal of a bell or the rolls of a drum, and at the invitation of the Town-cryer (*bandu-reader*) the members would proceed to the Loggia of the Parliament or to the cathedral hall.

There they deliberated about the taxes to be imposed; the safeguarding of long-held privileges, established customs and sacred traditions especially where these were perceived as being threatened by foreign overlords. The Commune would also demand an account of public officials and eventually they would list any complaints to bring them to the attention of the Viceroy, sometimes by sending envoys – as happened when Frederic IV visited Malta in 1372. And again when Martin the Elder was reported to be visiting Catania in 1409 – though he never did, having died before setting foot in Catania. But the Maltese could not have known that and a delegation had been sent to Catania to make representations to the King even though he was no longer the ruling monarch since he had abdicated in favour of his son Martin the Younger.

The other arm of the administrative system of government in

Malta was called the Consiglio Particolare and was made up of four Jurats (chosen by the Maltese parliament and approved by the king's representative), certain officials and some other special representatives from the Consiglio Popolare. This body did not have deliberative or legislative powers as we understand them today, but they proposed laws and made recommendations to the Feudal Lords who, at least as far as the interior affairs were concerned, usually granted them without too much hassle.

It must be remembered that although all this looks impressive and very nearly democratic on paper, in actual fact these were feudal times and the word of the monarch or his representative was law and could undo at one go whatever had been gained before.

2. The social classes

As to the social warp and woof of Maltese society: there was a very strict hierarchical system with the noble families, or those who had been elevated to that rank by the overlords, holding in fact the highest honours and titles and therefore the most authority simply on the basis of their nobility. These nobles amounted to about twenty families in all in the islands. In keeping with the feudal mentality that entrenched a very strong caste system, these were at the peak of the local pyramid and became *Milites* or *Notabiles*. The rank and file showed extreme deference to these people – and of course on their part the nobles did not fail to exact the same.

Lower down the social ladder, there were the divisions according to the artisan classes: priests, merchants, professionals. Then came the middle class and, finally, on the lowest rungs, the poorer classes. This tiered division prevailed even within the Church whose saints were divided into three categories according to their social background: a) the noble class (*nobilibus parentibus*), b) the middle class (*parentibus honestis*) and c) the lower or poor class (*parentibus pauperibus*).

The class-consciousness was so ingrained that we find that one of the requests made to the Sicilian Viceroy by the Maltese Commune was to abrogate the right of shoemakers, tailors and others like fishermen and cotton-weavers to be chosen for respectable assignments.

In the course of time, each artisan class as well as the professionals like the medical practitioners must have realized that like must help like and that people with similar interests were to join together to help each other for no other help was forthcoming from elsewhere. So each class began to form its own fraternity or guild, choosing some saint or other for a Patron.

Since there was no charter of rights or pensions, or health insurance, these guilds met together and donated funds to help their own kind, into which members of their guild/fraternity could dip in times of need.

All in all this very rigid caste-system which was hierarchical, despotic and autocratic was to leave its mark on Maltese society, whether civil or ecclesiastical, for many years to come. In fact it was exploited by all the present and successive overlords of Malta: Hospitallers, French, British and, eventually, Maltese themselves.

3. The Military defence of Malta

It bears remembering that the Anjevins, from their stronghold in Naples, had not given up hope, ever, of re-capturing Sicily and the islands i.e. Malta and Gozo and Pantelleria. In this they were abetted by their naval allies the Venetians and Genoese who kept their fleets roving close by, and by the popes who with their theocratic policy and their so-called *Patrimony of St Peter* wanted by all means to undermine Aragonese power in the Mediterranean. Added to all this, was the constant threat of corsairs at a time when piracy was a way of life, a very lucrative one and many powerful rulers in the Mediterranean fostered it because of the revenue it engendered for kingly coffers.

As such it behoved each country but more so the island-states, completely surrounded by water and hence extremely vulnerable, to make sure that they could defend their shores from marauders. It behoved Malta therefore to form and maintain its own defence system.

This took place in the shape of an outfit that came to be known locally as the *Dejma* – from the Maltese word *dejjem* which means *ever, always*, for such protectors had ever to be on alert and ready to defend at a moment's notice. (Shades of the Boy Scouts' motto: "be prepared").

At first the Dejma was made up of a volunteer force: people felt that defending their shores was a civic duty and an obvious necessity. Eventually when King Alfons gave the Maltese the right to bear arms in the defence of their country, conscription for the 18 to 60 year-old males became mandatory.

Besides, each citizen had to contribute towards the Dejma and its maintenance according to his status in society. Thus, the nobleman had to furnish for the construction and maintenance of the *felukkas* (sailing ships) as well as recruit sailors for the same. He had as well to supply combat horses and mares.

The heads of families had to keep lances, javelins, arrows, slings, swords in stock to wield as needed; and, after fire-power was introduced, such weapons as fire-arms as well.

The different families, under the command of a captain, were assigned various strategic points such as hills and critical stretches of shore-line or key posts all around Malta and Gozo and as soon as these sentries would see anything suspicious making its way to these shores, they would set the alarm – lighting a fire at night or making smoke during the day – and thus the whole island would be mobilized in its own self-defence.

The above was a blueprint for the way things were supposed to work, ideally. However, one comes across many instances when citizens tried to get out of sentry-duty by bribing officials (for example peasants who could not be bothered with wasting precious harvest-time scanning the horizon to detect the occasional enemy) with the expected results.

Occasionally there were particularly atrocious invasions such as the one in September 1429 when Kajd Ridavan is said to have attacked from Tunis with a fleet of 18,000 and besieged Malta in what has come to be known in local folklore as the Bread and Cheese Ploy and Counter Ploy. To insult the Maltese who had come to the end of their resistance after a particularly long siege, Kajd Ridavan had a number of loaves sent to the besieged. He wanted thereby to show to the Maltese that he was bent on winning fair and square and not because the defendants had come to the end of their resistance by being starved to death. The Maltese, wanting to pay the invaders in kind, sent the loaves back with a Maltese cheeselet (ġbejna) on top of each, returning the insult with thanks and signifying their intention to resist till the end unaided by enemy bribes.

On another occasion, in 1487, the fleet of the Turk Bajazet II entered Marsaxlokk and advanced right up to Borgo's *Castrum maris* with the sailors plundering away to their hearts' content along the way and taking a number of the local population into slavery. While in 1526 Rais Sinan Ciefut disembarked at Salini, marched to Mosta and took about 400 inhabitants into slavery.

In spite of these enemy forays and their daunting statistics many citizens tried to wangle out of their bounden duty to perform sentry or guard-duty (it must have been so boring, anyhow) with the result that there must have been many other minor and less sensational attacks that went unrecorded.

4. Daily life in the Maltese Islands

How did the Maltese in the time of the Aragonese overlords make their living? What were the primary modes of sustenance?

A great number of the inhabitants running into hundreds, were engaged in sentry or military duties as shown above. But what about the rest? What did they do?

In the order of priority, especially when it comes to revenue-earning, piracy took first place. This is natural, when one considers that the Maltese archipelago is surrounded by water and the distances to the next strips of land, north or south, are so great. Piracy was a public, governmental enterprise by means of which government could not only put to good use its own pirates to scare the enemy and keep it far from the local shores, but at the same time provide revenue for the public coffers by piracy-licences and the taxes imposed on the spoils.

There was also a wide gamut of ancillary industries related to piracy. Carpenters were needed for the very extensive wood work in boat building; smiths for the making of all the equipment needed for fighting in terms of weapons, swords and so on; sail-making; masonry in the building of watch-towers and castles all round the islands and a host of other things. No wonder that the Maltese along with the Greeks, Sardinians and Genoese were considered among the best pirates in the Mediterranean right up till the 18th century.

As we have seen it was the duty of the noble families to see to the building as well as the furnishing of sailing vessels which had to be manned by expert crews. And the Maltese made excellent sailors.

The Maltese pirates who actually roamed the seas had to get a licence from the Vice-Admiral of Sicily who also assigned the fishing grounds and insisted on the ban on foraging on Christian ships (which oddly included Greek Orthodox and more oddly Jewish). They were limited and obliged to plunder only enemy ships, i.e. those of Moslems, whether Arab or Turk made no difference. As is to be expected, a whole set of myths and legends grew up about the exploits of these audacious and daring Maltese pirates and many of them have passed into local folklore.

However, there were other industries, besides piracy, to keep the local populace busily engaged. For those who were more agriculturally inclined, there was the tending of the olive-trees and the harvesting of the olives, along with the olive-oil industry that flourished with it.

There was also the cultivation and harvesting of cotton – a plant that was very much sought after for so many necessities of life such as clothing starting with headgear down to shirts and pants. Another industry was the cultivation of the herb cumin as well as vines for wine-making.

5. Church life

What about the religious scene in Malta under the Aragonese? First of all this was the age in Christianity that saw the founding of many new, as well as the flourishing of the old Religious Orders, both male and female, in the whole of Europe. As such there was an influx of these same religious orders into Malta – which happened mostly between 1370 and 1495.

Thus during this period we find the Franciscans near the Hospital of Sancto Spiritu in Rabat; the Carmelites just outside Rabat at the Church of Lunzjata; the Augustinians just outside Mdina at the present site of Howard's Gardens and then at Saqqajja; the Dominicans at Our Lady of the Cave; the Benedictines and so on. These monks and religious were mostly involved in education, primarily the teaching of Christian doctrine especially in the spacious convents attached to parishes. Being the ones with a better education, the friars often ended up being the notaries, teachers and in general, the people most looked up to and most respected on the islands.

However, there was currently in Europe antagonism between two very strong elements, a carry-over from the Guelph and Ghibelline tussle of earlier times – one pro-pope and the other anti-pope. This acrimony was further aggravated now because there was a long period of time when there was confusion in the papacy: Christianity even had an anti-pope and the House of Aragon – to

The Carmelite "hermitage" at Lunzjata was one of the earliest to be set up here in Malta

whom Malta belonged – embraced a civil and ecclesiastical policy that tried to wean itself from popish influence.

The various popes did not hide their favourable leanings towards the Anjevins and the House of Anjou. As such, they also kept up their unceasing efforts, as we have seen, to re-establish the Anjevins in Sicily and Malta. The result was that in Malta, too, the clergy and the people – most of whom followed the lead of their clergy – were split. So much so that when the bishopric became vacant, some Maltese canons (residing in Catania) nominated as their bishop, John of Pino who was a follower of the anti-Pope, thereby pleasing the Aragon king. The Maltese canons in Malta however, chose the Benedictine Dom Mauro Calì and there is no need to say that the Pope, in a (papal) bull sent to the Cathedral chapter at Mdina, confirmed the latter.

The uncertainty and downright apprehension in the local religious scene was further enhanced by the fact that the first rumblings of the inquisitorial type of faith enforcement began to be felt on the islands at this time as well, though, as we shall see, the full-fledged power of the Roman Inquisition in all its ramifications in Malta does not materialize until the arrival and full entrenchment of the Knights Hospitallers of St John of Jerusalem.

The winds of Change

If one were to try to formulate an overall impression that marked the Aragonese presence in the Kingdom of Sicily and hence by association in Malta, one must say that their two and a half-centuries here were characterized by brutal and callous dealings. Under the Aragonese, the Kingdom of Sicily – and hence the Maltese Islands – pass from one hand to another, from one feudal lord to another, as convenience and circumstances dictate without any regard being had for the allegiance or feelings of the people involved. The disposal of such fiefdoms at the will of the monarch or feudal overlord to anybody he pleases usually brought about a lot of suffering and distress among the subject-peoples for the feudal lords were more keen on exacting taxes, reaping profits and garnering wealth for themselves from their subjects than in improving the lot of their subjects and still less did they bother about remedying any complaints.

In fact, many a time, the Maltese Islands ended up being bartered and exchanged with never a hoot being given to the wishes of the people. The result was a feeling of helplessness: if all this could happen to a much bigger island, Sicily, all the more it could happen to the Maltese islands.

Accustomed as they were to being shuffled around from one owner to another, the Maltese were not surprised, though not necessarily happy, when they eventually found themselves and their islands being deeded to a new Mediterranean superpower: the Knights Hospitallers of St John of Jerusalem.

This Christian Religious Order of military monks had been ousted from their seat of power, the Holy Land and in successive unseatings, from their places of refuge: Acre, Cyprus and Rhodes.

They went about Europe seeking a home and a place in which they could settle. They went around Europe – to Francis the King of France since the majority of the knights were French. But Francis was more keen on allying himself with the Moslem Suleiman to invade the fellow-Christian but mighty enemy King Charles of Spain. They went to Henry VIII in England who was already engaged in his papal battles with Rome over his marriages and who was not too keen on helping an outfit that had a special vow of allegiance to Rome.

In the end and in desperation, they went to Charles I of Spain. This monarch had brought under his rule the dynasties of Aragon, Castile and Burgundy as well as the Austrian possessions of the House of Hapsburg, the Netherlands, Luxembourg, Sardinia, Sicily, the greater parts of Italy, and Spanish conquests in North Africa and the New World. He was also the Emperor of the Holy Roman Empire (as Charles V) and so found it in his heart, with some nudging from the Holy Father, to grant them the islands of Malta and Gozo for their headquarters – especially since the Knights had settled in Catania on a temporary *pied-a-terre* and Charles was not too keen on letting the Knights interfere with the administration of that big island.

And so Malta and Gozo passed into the hands of the Knights Hospitallers of St John of Jerusalem, or rather the *Castellum maris* at Borgo was ceded to them as the locale for their new quarters – a move that was to link inexorably Malta's fate with that of the Knights, another set of new settlers, for the next 270 years.

Chapter 9

The Age of Celibate Gentlemen of Chivalry: The Knights Hospitallers of St John of Jerusalem

(1530–1798)

In May 1530 a decree was signed by Charles V that ceded Malta to the now homeless and stateless Religious Order of military monks known as the Knights Hospitallers of St John of Jerusalem. Charles V could very well do this because he was the Head of the Holy Roman Empire and his domain included besides Spain, the Netherlands, Germany, Sardinia, the Kingdom of the Two Sicilies (of which Malta at the time formed part) as well as the newly-conquered territories in New Spain. In fact, the Holy Roman Empire, created to replace the old Constantinian and Carolingian Empires embraced most of the then known world: faithful Christian as well as infidel nations. Under him came duchies, countries and bishoprics owing formal allegiance to the Emperor. As such, Charles V was expected to come to the rescue of this most worthy Religious Order of vowed warrior-knight Hospitallers who, so they claimed, had merited so well of Christianity to date.

Charles V was expected to be generous especially since some friendly though authoritative nudging came from the Occupier of the Throne of Peter who at the time besides being Supreme Spiritual Leader of Christianity, was also Temporal Head of the Papal States. And especially since other Heads of State, equally Christian – such as England and France – could not be bothered with such an outfit as the Hospitallers. They kept themselves busy with their petty feuds at home or with fighting one another, or with Rome. There were other reasons which deterred Catholic monarchs from coming to the Hospitallers' rescue such as the very real fear of the very real power they wielded. Many monarchs had second thoughts too because of the Hopsitallers' track record: their autocratic form of government could become in due time a threat to royal power once they gained a foothold.

How did the Knights Hospitallers end up homeless and stateless and why was Malta given to them as their new headquarters?

The historical background

When, back in 1099, in Jerusalem a certain Gerard became head of a brotherhood whose main purpose was to provide *hospitium* (shelter) even as the brothers ministered to and assisted the exhausted, wounded and dying Christian pilgrims (mostly from Western Europe) who came on pilgrimage to the Holy Land, the seed for this Fraternity had been sown.

These pilgrims, having traversed the whole of Europe to make this very difficult pilgrimage, most often ended up waylaid, beaten, exhausted, sick and often killed by friends (Oriental: Byzantine, Greek Christians) and foes (Moslems, nomads) alike. To the ailing pilgrims there were added the wounded and dying Crusaders once the Crusades got under way – and hence the crying need for a nursing fraternity to take care of the sick and dying. The Hospitallers had their work cut out for them.

In the *glorious* period of the Crusades (1095-1272), Popes like Urban II as well as fire-brand preachers like Peter the Hermit and Bernard of Clairvaux had incited the Christians of Europe to wars of liberation – to free from the yoke of the Moslem domination, considered infidel – that Land so dear to Christianity, Palestine. This meant that it was up to the Christian Nobles of Europe to lead their Christian subjects in such Crusades of liberation.

However, the Moslem world also considered this land holy to its own memory, one of the great pilgrim-sites of their Moslem faith in fact, especially because of the Prophet's sojourn there and his ascent into heaven from the Holy City of Jerusalem. The Moslems were not about to give up that land, once acquired, without a fight. The Jews, who by right had prior claim to it all, did not even enter into the equation at this time, because this was the time of the *Diaspora* – they were in exile all over the rest of the world.

So, paradoxically, Palestine, made holy by the presence of Christ, the Prince of Peace for Christians, and Mohamet the peaceful Prophet of Islam became the bone of contention among the respective followers of these two religions. To the Christians, Palestine had to be wrested away from the domination of the *infidels* whether Moslem or otherwise – even though for the Moslems this was equally holy territory and, especially in the eyes of the Moslem Turkish dynasties that ruled Palestine most of the time, a valuable piece of real estate as well to add to the list of conquered territories.

Eventually therefore, on the Christian side, various groups of men and women were formed who banded together and, as was wont with religious groups at the time, vowed perpetual poverty, chastity and obedience along with, in the case of the hospitaller orders, special hospitality service to the visiting pilgrims who were wounded or became sick as they wended their way in pilgrimage to the Holy Land – or as they fought off enemies, human and animal, along the way.

The origins of the Hospitaller and other Orders

One such Order was the Knights Hospitallers of St John of Jerusalem. When Baldwin I, King of Jerusalem recognized the brotherhood in 1104 and Pope Paschal II sanctioned their statutes by a Papal Bull in 1113, the Hospitallers were well and truly established. (Both the original charter and the papal bull are to be found in Malta).

The 'Bulla' of Pope Paschal II establishing the order

On the Christian side, though, the Hospitallers were by no means the only ones so to organize. There were other groups of men: a fraternity that came to be known as the Knights of the Holy Sepulchre took its name from their original meeting-place, the Holy Sepulchre – the Temple built on Golgotha that enclosed both the crucifixion site and the Tomb of Christ. Eventually these knights came to be known as the Knight Templars and were in time to become competitors of the Hospitallers – unto death. Literally so.

A third group of Christians from the German-speaking lands also formed a confraternity that catered to the German-speaking pilgrims. These came to be known as the Teutonic Knights.

A number of legends about auspicious deeds of knights as they made their way to the Holy Land or on arrival there – on the lines of King Richard of England dubbed the Lion-hearted – fuelled the Christian imagination. Much of it, of course, was embellished in the re-telling. But it served the purpose of galvanizing Christian Europe against the enemy and all for a holy and worthy cause: the liberation and emancipation of the Holy Land from the hands and domination of the enemy.

However, all these religious groups soon discovered that turning the other cheek (as Christ had advised) was not always the accepted policy that provided safe-passage anywhere, least of all through hostile territory. So they combined the two aspects of religion and arms: they took religious vows along with the commission of militarily defending the pilgrims – by force of arms if need be. They became military monks: the brothers-in-religion became brothers-in-arms as well.

The fact that most of the members of the Orders came from the noble families of Europe who were both extremely wealthy and chivalry-minded gave further impetus to the military aspect of honour, as well as to the amassing of possessions.

Now to their own personal wealth was added that of the grateful pilgrims so ably tended to by these nursing communities. These pilgrims often ended up bequeathing their wealth to the Orders. All this, coupled with the wealth of their own members who themselves hailed from the affluent noble families of Europe to start with, in due time brought so much material prosperity and possessions to these Orders, that it all inevitably engendered a lot of enmity and envy and conflicts among them all, the very same Orders; as well as among those Catholic monarchs who were in a position to deprive them of some of it. Not to mention the temptation of their eternal enemies, the Moslem Turks and others – to make all this loot their own by claiming prior rights to it all. To which must be added the antagonism, ever since the schism in 1054, of the Greek Orthodox Church based in Constantinople (modern Istanbul). The balance of power often witnessed a see-saw alliance between Moslems, Orthodox and Catholics each trying to outdo and hoodwink the other/s with unholy alliances.

Of special fascinating historical interest is the inter-locking of claims that came to cross purposes and an eventual do-or-die struggle for survival among all these religious orders in the 13th century and which saw the squelching of the Knights Templars through diplomatic double-dealing and intrigue on the part of the European (Christian) powers of the time, thereby forcing the Pope to the deed – the papal *fiat* that brought about the dissolution of the Templars.

Still and all, at this period of time, in spite of having swallowed up their competition the Knights Templars, the Knights Hospitallers were not as mighty militarily as one would expect. Affluence may have been one very big reason. The tarnishing of their original *raison d'etre* another. The fact is that they suffered one humiliating defeat after another at the hands of the Moslem Turks both in the Holy Land and outside.

In fact, in 1187, having been hounded out of Jerusalem – which had been the Hospitaller home and headquarters for close to a century – they were forced into exile in Acre, when the Moslem Turks took control of the Holy Land (then called Palestine).

Even in Acre, though, they were not safe: the Moslem Turks followed and hounded them. And in 1291 the Knights Hospitallers sought refuge in Cyprus. But this was not adequate to their needs. In 1309-10 they found a home in the Island of Rhodes where they survived till 1522.

However, the Moslem Turkish Empire had become strong enough to dictate matters and could brook no competition in the Mediterranean, their theatre of operations. The Turks followed the Hospitallers to Rhodes as well and, after a long and heroic siege, the Knights had to abandon Rhodes too.

Hospitaller historians narrate that the enemy (the Moslem Turks) was so impressed with the resistance the Knights had put up in spite of the siege, that, in true and proper admiration of chivalry, they gave the Knights a royal send-off from Rhodes and allowed them to take most of their prized possessions with them. We only have the Hospitaller side of the story about this, though and hence objective confirmation from a neutral source is not available.

It was 1522 – and the Knights of the once mighty Hospitaller Order were now homeless and stateless.

The Hospitallers in Malta

And that is when they ended up roaming all over Europe – trying to find a country that would grant them asylum and a place to call home and in which to establish their new headquarters, which is when they ended up in Malta, being given this plot of land as a fiefdom by Charles V.

Soon they moved to their quarters in Borgo (modern-day Birgu) where the Grand Master could have a better view of the harbour and surrounding country-side from a proper magisterial palace duly built and protected by impressive bastions.

Malta, it must be remembered, had its own government which at the time consisted in the so-called **Commune** and the *Università*

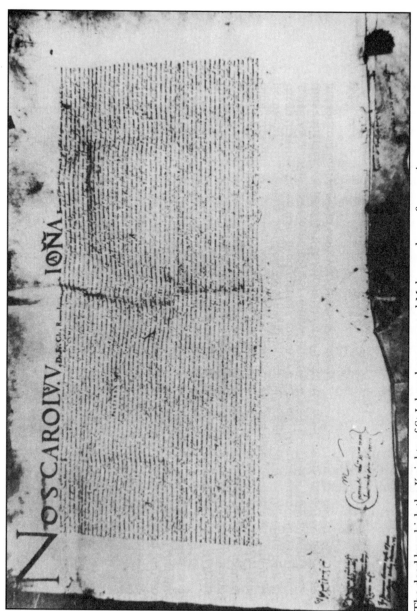

The deed by which the Knights of St John where granted Malta as a base of operations

as we have seen – more like a management-taxation bureau – in the hands of the local Nobility as per medieval fiefdom tradition.

With the arrival of the Knights Hospitallers, Malta became an overcrowded little enclave with two super-powers: one local and one international in a few square miles of rock, and fewer still of arable land, but without all that much wealth in natural resources to make up for the lack of space. Very soon, with the the establishment of the Inquisition and the appointment of an Inquisitor, Malta became the base of a three-fold tussle – which complicated matters terribly.

It is with all this in mind that the arrival of the Knights in Malta under their Grand Master Fra Philippe Villiers de L'Isle Adam in October of 1530 has to be viewed – an event that did not go down well with the local Nobility who were not consulted about these new (and unwelcome) additions to the island and who were indeed considered as a definite threat to their power. Such a foreign outfit was bound to bring new imported ideas to upset the established *status quo* prevalent here. Yet another foreign power to dictate matters to the local nobles.

A touchy situation that was further aggravated by the Grand Master who insisted on formally taking possession of the islands by a solemn entry into the seat of power: Mdina.

The Knights at their Borgo phase

Whatever one says about the Knights Hospitallers of St John of Jerusalem at this stage, about their arrival in Malta this much is clear: they were resented as intruders by the governing body. And this for many reasons. First of all they had negotiated their coming to Malta with the Holy Roman Emperor Charles V behind the back of the local feudal barons who were not even consulted in the matter. Once in Malta, they brought with them a very strong aristocratic-autocratic form of government with a direct line of communication to all the Noble Dynasties of Europe and most definitely to the Pope in Rome. Their monarchic ambitions hailed their Grand Master as

The Knights first settled in Borgo – making the Parish Church their Conventual Church

Prince and Most Illustrious which he was – in an autocratic-despotic sort of way. The Hospitallers lorded it over all they saw and everything they espied and looked with disdain on the local nobility already entrenched and in power in Malta.

The Hospitallers had a very efficient, self-contained form of government – including their own courts and jail – that controlled everything within the Order and tried to influence everything outside its perimeters. They looked down on the local people with whom they never mixed socially. As to the common people, these had no say at all in government and were looked upon as cheap labour, along with the slaves, for the many various projects that needed doing. This was evident in their Borgo-phase (1530 to 1571) but more so in their Valletta-phase (up to 1798). How did they do this and what was this form of government of the Hospitaller Order?

The Form of Hospitaller Government

As a Religious Order (monks with vows of obedience, poverty and chastity) of aristrocratic members hailing from the most affluent and noble families of Europe, the Order believed primarily in a hierarchy of powers and honours.

As to government, there were various stages of development. It was malleable enough to circumstances so that various instruments of government were created as need arose so that eventually it came to be governed by four different Councils: the Complete, the Ordinary, the Secret and the Criminal.

The Supreme Authority within the Order was vested in a council, the complete council, presided over by the Grand Master or his Lieutenant that met for all extraordinary matters such as the election of a Grand Master, declaration of war etc.

The Ordinary Venerable Council of the Sixteen met with the Grand Master to discuss and decide all the daily matters dealing with the running of the Order. This elite group was made up of the

Eight Heads of the *langues*, (langue: a linguistic group living in an *auberge* or barracks), and their Lieutenants.

The Secret Council, as the name implies, dealt with sensitive matters of State to which only trusted members could be privy. It covered all the diplomatic relations with other nations, (a sort of Foreign Affairs Ministry) and was a later creation of the Hospitaller sojourn in Malta.

The Criminal Council dealt with all matters relating to the Order's internal discipline. It had the power even to send to jail any member of the Order who was so sentenced. Various members, including Grand Masters themselves (e.g. de la Cassiere) were sent to prison – sometimes due to rank-and-file mutinies against the Grand Master. Duelling – which was a common though forbidden way to settle quarrels among those to the rapier born – was also an offence punishable by jail terms when the perpetrators were caught and brought to Court.

Membership

To join the Order, a candidate had to prove and provide documents of his nobility to the quaternary degree (both sides of grandparents). He joined as a novice for a year in the Auberge (barracks/hostel) of his Langue and then, depending on his aristocratic rank and achievements within the Order, he could rise to one of three grades: Knight of Justice (*Miles*, i.e. Military knight); or Knight of Honour and Devotion; or Knight of Magistral Grace.

There were also Knights Chaplains who ministered to the spiritual needs of the monk-knights. Even here there was a hierarchy of self-contained pyramidal order with a Grand Prior, various ranks of chaplains, of which the Conventual Chaplain was the most prestigious.

Finally came the Donats or Servants-at-arms who were auxiliaries – not essential to the Order but very convenient helpers.

As to their provenance, the knights, the pick of European nobility, hailed from different countries in Europe. And as such, each big block was represented by a Langue or Language-group. The members of each Langue residing in their respective auberge had their own distinguishing banner, coat-of-arms and uniform. Each Langue had its specific role within the Order as well. At their arrival in Malta, these roles were quite clearly defined because, in fact, they had been created for some specific purpose in the total war-machine of defence against the Turks. In the Malta phase, some langues even spawned off-shoots to adjust to changed circumstances e.g. the suppression of the Order in England under Henry VIII brought about the near-demise of the English Langue; while changed circumstances brought about the amalgamation of Portugal and Castile.

The Langues

There were different langues at different times, but at its most glorious the Order had eight major ones, which followed again a hierarchy of seniority, depending on when they were founded.

1) The Langue of Provence was the oldest, hence seniormost

The Grand Commandeur or Head, known as the Grand Preceptor was the Chief Treasurer of the Order. Knights from this nation were entrusted with anything to do with the administration of property of the far-flung Hospitaller empire known as the *Aerarium Commune* or Common Treasury: moneys, minting of coins and commemorative medals at the accession of a new Grand Master, etc.

The Order had properties abroad in the shape of priories, commanderies and bailiwicks, and various members of the Order were appointed to such titles and benefices, usually as a reward for a particular feat of valour or for being instrumental in bringing added riches to the Order in the shape of loot from sea-forays in the Mediterranean where pirate or Turkish ships were the preferred targets. The Order had a lot of wealth also which was measured in the number of slaves – in which it did a thriving business. As well as *bona voglia* (lit: good will, i.e. volunteer) workers such as oarsmen for the many ships who were paid – sometimes.

2) The Langue of Auvergne

Its Head was called the Grand Marshal for this langue was entrusted with the control of the military administration which was quite involved and extensive – as befitted a military order.

3) The Langue of France

This country (not the same boundaries of the France of today) was among the most glorious for it fulfilled the specific role for which originally the Order was founded i.e. caring for the sick. Its Head was Chief Hospitaller and he supervised the running of the Sacred Infirmary i.e. hospital, and trained the recruits that came from France in hospital work.

4) The Langue of Italy

It was entrusted with the care of the Order's Fleet, so the head was the Admiral and had the custody of anything related to navigation, navy, convoys, flotilla-movements as well as ship-building and shipyarding.

5) The Langue of Aragon

The Head was known as the Grand Conservator for this nation was in charge of supplies, and made sure that all possible supplies for fleet as well as the military movements were available as and when needed. It took care of all the logistics for all this as well as the provisions necessary in food, equipment, ammunitions and materiel for clothing down even to the cloth for sails for the fleet. It was eventually split up:

6) The Langue of Castille and Leon (to which in time Portugal was joined)

This had as its Head the Chancellor and it was the one that supplied all the scribes of the Order. In an age when few people could read or write, most knights (including many Grand Masters) were illiterate and so the Chancery and its scribes played a very key role. It provided all the clerks, secretaries, notaries for deed-writing, aides as well as dictation-takers for all occasions.

The members of the Langue of Castille, Leon and Portugal were the ones who also provided the written reports of all the Conciliar sessions the Grand Master held with his Councils. These have come to be known as *Libri Conciliorum* (Books of the Councils) and which are the detailed, day-to-day hand-written journals of all that took place within the Order and in its relations with the Maltese authorities – an invaluable insight into the inner workings of the Order as well as of contemporary life in Malta.

These secretaries were also responsible for the keeping of the records of the progeny of the knights – no mean feat when we remember that each knight had to supply proofs of quaternary nobility from both sides of his grandparents. They also kept records of the supplies, warehousing and property of the Order in its far-flung empire.

7) The Langue of Germany

The Head of this langue who styled himself as Grand Bailiff was responsible for the fortifications: the building and maintenance of the bastions, warehouses, chapels and Churches of the Order and all such buildings.

8) The Langue of England

Its head was known as the Turcopilier i.e. the Fender-off of the Turks because he commanded the Christian janissaries and undertook as well the total control of the mounted forces and the coastguard. An English knight, Oliver Starkey became famous as the Secretary of Grand Master La Vallette.

This much for the Hospitaller Order and its administrative departments. Naturally, we are systematizing here in a schematic way what took shape over a very long period of time because when they landed in Malta, the Knights Hospitallers were not as yet so well-organized as all this. But true military and disciplined Order that they were, they soon set about making themselves at home on this little tongue of land called Borgo, setting up the various auberges, building the fortifications, constructing the Grand Magisterial Palace that is still a pleasant marvel today and ... waiting for their eternal enemy, the Moslem Turk that did not take long to come and was to make the Order famous for the Great Siege that lasted for most of the year 1565.

It was probably due to this claim to fame that under the British, the ex-headquarters of the Hospitallers now re-named Fort St Angelo, served as the Headquarters for the Admiral of the Mediterranean Fleet and was a nerve-centre during the Second World War.

The Roman Inquisition in Malta

Although we find references to Pro-Inquisitors in the islands of Malta and Gozo in the century previous to the Knights Hospitallers' arrival in Malta, it is only after their arrival here that the Inquisition makes its full-strength appearance in Malta. But first of all a brief word about this institution.

In general the Inquisition was a judicial tribunal and was instituted by the Popes in Rome to foster the teachings of the Catholic Church and safeguard and protect same from any possibility of distortion or error by unorthodox believers. At times the co-operation of the Catholic monarchs was added to the weight of the Inquisitor who was the representative of the Pope in any particular country.

The Inquisition was of three kinds: the Medieval, the Spanish and the Roman. The first, the Medieval is purported to have been set up by Pope Lucius III in 1184 and reinforced in the Council of Lateran (1215) with the latter's insistence on exterminating the Catharic and Albigensian heresies. The second type, the Spanish Inquisition was set up by Pope Sixtus, in 1478, precisely during the Aragonese domination in Europe's history at the request of King Ferdinand of Aragon and Queen Isabella of Castille. Its main aim was to bring to trial those *Maranos* Jews in Spain who to save their skin and under the guise of being baptized had retained, deep down, their Jewish faith. This is one of the darkest pages of anti-semiticism in the history of Christian Europe. It was a political as well as a religious tribunal and fell to such depths as condemning the sale of horses and munitions to France as being seditiously non-Christian.

The third brand of Inquisition was the Roman and it was set up in 1542 by Pope Paul III by the papal bull he promulgated *Licet ab initio* (*Although from the beginning*).

Mercifully, historians aver, it was the Roman and not the Spanish Inquisitorial brand that prevailed here in Malta. Still it was the Inquisition, and though at first there were a number of fumbling mistakes because of overlapping of jurisdiction (inquisitorial, Hospitaller and episcopal), eventually the various areas of competence and authority were ironed out.

Thus, by the end of the 16th century, the Inquisitor is given by Rome plenipotentiary powers as to the moral as well as spiritual and material fields. He is also made the personal representative of the Holy Father in Malta and as such claiming absolute jurisdiction over all that happened in the islands.

This reinforcement and re-alignment of powers created a lot of friction with the Knights Hospitallers. Being used to absolute power themselves they viewed the Inquisitor as an intrusion and a curbing of their absolute hegemony.

This difference of views was the start of a diplomatic as well as a religious power struggle that was to last for the duration of the Hospitallers' stay in Malta.

To start with, since they were a self-contained community with their own Law courts, the Knights presumed that any time any of their Order's members went on their errant ways, their own system of justice would see to the addressing of the issues and the punishment of the culprits in question. For another, since the Grand Master was the absolute ruler of the islands, equal in rank to a Cardinal, it was he, along with the Hospitallers' Venerable Council, who should be the one to have the final say and decision in any matter within his territory.

On top of it all, the highest clerical rank within the Order was a Grand Prior while often the Inquisitor, though a Cleric, was no more than a Notary or Legal Apostolic Official, or, at most, a J.U.C. (Canon and Civil Lawyer) and very rarely even ordained priest.

No need to say, these divergent ideas of authority and jurisdiction brought about a very definite tussle of powers, for the Inquisitors, housed in a palace in Borgo, took their function seriously.

It was the primary duty and assignment of the Inquisition, in its 200-year presence in Malta, to see to it that each little and big injunction of evangelical and Church practice was faithfully observed here. Thus not only was Mass on Sundays and Feasts of Obligation to be meticulously attended by each and every Catholic, but also the days of fast and abstinence had to be observed. None of the Church laws was to be flouted – at least no one should get the impression he could get away with it.

But more than this, the Inquisition was here to safeguard the orthodoxy of Church doctrine from the theological and heretical errors that other North European countries had shamefacedly fallen into. And so in Malta, the Knights and the Maltese were encouraged to spy on each other and report any real or suspected straying from the right path.

The Inquisition in Malta kept everybody on the straight and narrow

Not only that, it was made incumbent under pain of sin – and torture, when caught – that such divulging was one's sacred duty to God and country.

One can only imagine what a hot-bed of tattle-tale, false accusations, and rampant injustices such a mentality brought about with each one spying on the other and being obliged to report any least deviation, suspected or real, from the Faith or the day-to-day practice.

What were the great sins prevalent at the time and on which the Inquisition pounced with vigour?

One was witchcraft and necromancy. And this was intolerable because it was a form of stranglehold that threatened the very official authority itself.

Another was prostitution. A number of Inquisitors complained about this wound in Maltese society which was often mostly nourished by the very Knights themselves. In fact, they had brought over their camp-followers from Rhodes to Malta! And once established here, the business flourished mostly among the Hospitallers themselves. The amount of illegitimate issue that such unions brought about can only be surmized – which added still further to the ethnic and racial mix on the islands!

Added to all this was the practice of taking God's name in vain – blasphemy – which has been a bane on the islands from forever it seems; as well as making light of one's faith.

But mostly, the Inquisitors complained about the lack of observance of protocol on the part of the Knights who suffered them badly. The Knights considered themselves supreme authority on the island and they would find any least breach of protocol as good an excuse as any to rub it in, by methods ranging from the petty to the sublime: the Grand Master would overlook paying his courtesy visit to the Inquisitor on the latter's arrival from Rome; the kneelers at respite stops during processions (like those of the Blessed

Sacrament on Corpus Christi) would be placed so that the Inquisitor's would be lower than the Grand Master's; the Knights would forget to invite the Inquisitor for official ceremonies at their conventual Church; inquisitorial secret mail sent to Rome via the Order's galleys would mysteriously come apart and open up for inspection.

Mostly it was a cat and mouse game of a struggle for power and control.

As time went on and the Inquisitor was well and truly established, further galling differences ensued. The Inquisitor needed a number of employees to help him in his work. So he granted such inquisitorial employees the privilege of *patent*.

Such persons would become automatically and directly subject to Inquisitorial jurisdiction alone and exempt from the Hospitaller sphere of authority. This did not sit well with the supreme authority which the Knights claimed over the whole of Malta. And when an increasing number of Maltese noblemen and clergy, disgruntled at the Hospitaller authoritarian mode of government sought immunity by buying off such patenting, the tussle between Inquisition and Hospitaller Order came to a head!

Not that the Inquisitor was granted a free hand even in the conduct of his inquisitorial affairs: many big and small decisions had to be taken by Rome, for the Holy Father and his various Congregations held the strings to all of the Christian subjects throughout the world and *a fortiori* to their Tribunal representatives.

Such subjection as is unthinkable for us today, even in our era of modern communications was, back then, the way of doing things. Each and every decision, even those relating to the punishment for inquisitorial offences, had to be approved by Rome. And when one considers the time it took for vessels to go to Rome and come back, one realizes the inconveniences to the accused, not to say the outright injustices such a system entailed.

However, the Inquisitors were mostly Church-men on their way up the ecclesiastical-honours ladder and servile adherence to superiors was one surefire blueprint for success and further advancement. In fact many of the Inquisitors who served in Malta went on to further accolades as bishops, cardinals and even popes.

Why were Church honours so sought after? In a sort of literal application of the biblical *the worker being worthy of his wages*, these Church honours were accompanied by appropriate benefices: a sort of steady and sure revenue concomitant with the job. In an age when work benefits, sick leave and pensions were unheard of, a cleric could rest assured that his present and future were taken care of if he garnered some such benefice. And he could garner same if he followed the strict lines of obedient non-questioning to authority and hence, referral of all things to the authorities in Rome.

In due time and as the heretical errors made their way through Europe, Rome became more defensive still. Torture of the most horrible kind (even though by some historians not as extreme as that practised by the Spanish Inquisition) would extort any and all confessions from debilitated victims.

That heretical errors managed to infiltrate here as well, in spite of the bastion-mentality (both physical and mental) prevailing in Malta is surprising – though given the elite and effete aristocracy of Europe represented by the Knights in these islands, this was inevitable.

For many decades, one such big underground enemy was free-masonry. The lodge was established in Malta mostly due to the French knights who brought these freemason ideas from their homeland. Meetings were held in various spots in Malta, purportedly for the first time in the 1740's – and ever since then, masons have been firmly and truly established here in spite of Church condemnation and prohibition, and even though masonic teaching was equated with demoniac seances.

Another sore point about the Inquisition in Malta is that although the Inquisitors were here to supervize morality, they themselves were not always above reproach morally-speaking and some even sired illegitimate off-spring from liaisons with Maltese women. It must be said that though all the Inquisitors were clerics and as such bound by the vows of celibacy not all were ordained priests. For many, Malta was a trial ground of their virtues, and especially for their ingenuity to overcome the boredom of the place. Apparently court sessions, flogging, tongs, running needles through tongues, condemning to the 'saddle', sentencing to darkened jails – none of this provided enough diversion. Many inquisitors yearned for the fame that assignment back to civilization, especially in the centre of Christianity, Rome, would bring them.

Many Inquisitors considered their sojourn in Malta as one of trial and penance in a god-forsaken outpost that was so far away from the centre of the world: Rome. One positive outcome of all this: perhaps due to this very boredom they experienced, the Inquisitors had all the time in the world to meticulously record all of the many cases that came up before the Inquisitorial Court and Malta is lucky enough to have all of its inquisitorial records safely archived. They are also lucky to have been preserved intact, having avoided the frenzied destiny of Napoleonic destruction that such documents suffered when visited by this dictator in other countries. Luckily, historians are provided with a welter of material about contemporary life in Malta as well as Inquisitorial procedural methods. All of these documents of course, were meant for the Inquisitors' eyes only. Another plus for historians here in Malta who can delve into very secret and personal material.

Another inquisitorial bequest – of questionable value this time, can be found in the petty-minded, eavesdropping, spying mentality that had been sown in Malta and of which the Maltese have been victims ever since.

The Government of Malta: the 'Università'

With two very vociferous bodies claiming hegemony over these small islands and fighting for supremacy among themselves, we tend to forget that there was a third force in Malta, that of the local government which anticipated them both – as we have seen under the Aragonese – and, often, resented them still more. This was known as the *Università dei grani* which as the name implies cared mostly for the provisions of food.

This was a regular (feudal) sort of government with the Mayor and his councillors – residing at Mdina, the 'old capital' and the original one.

This 'Università' was made up of noblemen living in Malta (some Maltese but also foreign ones) who had been set up as such by the King of Spain under whom Malta fell as it formed part of the Kingdom of the Two Sicilies (Naples and Sicily). They were engaged in collecting taxes – mostly in kind such as grain – and ware-housing same; in charging harbour fees for vessels entering the harbour; in fending off pirate attacks on the coastal villages and farms; and in recruiting able-bodied men to fight in the 'armed' forces that would see to the defence of Malta from the intruder and the defence of law from the law-breaker.

They would do all this by holding regular meetings in the Town Hall.

With the advent of the Hospitallers, many of these functions were taken over by the Knights. For a start, the Knights' coming to Malta attracted the Turks who were just as determined to undercut the Knights' naval supremacy in the Mediterranean and declare themselves rid of this opposition to their dream of total world domination once and for all. (Whoever controlled the Mediterranean, it must be remembered, controlled the then known civilized world.)

However, the Knights were equally determined to retain their hegemony – mostly because it was lucrative and brought them untold loot in the shape of captured enemy ships and, in an age where slavery was a measure of wealth, untold numbers of slaves. For slaves were used for all sorts of chores: from serving at table, to carrying letters, to helping build monumental masterpieces like palaces and Churches.

And with the attraction of the Turkish enemy to the shores of Malta, the Hospitaller Order had to bolster its defences and strengthen its forces – round its own perimeters. One such means was to recruit the Maltese workers in this enterprise – as oarsmen in the galleys; as orderlies at war; as attendants at hospitals, as donats to the men-at-arms, and in various other menial jobs. All of which, naturally, did not go down at all well with the 'Università'! For one thing it was a drain on the work-pool available. On the other it was a direct threat to and undermining of their authority!

And this tussle back and forth between the Università and the Hospitaller Order went on as long as the Order was in Malta. In fact, it was due to the dissatisfaction of the local gentry with the Order that eventually the latter saw their chance when Napoleon Buonaparte, anxious in his turn to take control of the world by controlling the Mediterranean, hovered long enough around Malta in the late 18th century. The disgruntled Maltese gentry saw their chance of getting rid of the Hospitallers and tilted the balance in favour of franco-philism.

History was to prove that they were to regret this move as well!

The Great Siege and its aftermath

As was to be expected, the Knights' arrival in Malta soon attracted the attention of their immortal and eternal enemies: the Turkish Sultans and their fleets and armies. These were very eager to see this Christian-European obstacle to their Turkish-Moslem dominance of the Mediteranean in the middle of this Basin done away with. The slave-trade could brook no competition. Nor could piracy of the Mediterranean high seas. Nor could, eventually, a religious philosophy that was at odds with that of its mortal enemies.

And so the Moslem-Turks began amassing their fleet and their soldiers and their prized warriors to mount an offensive against Malta that took months in the planning and longer in execution. They figured that if they enclosed the Knights Hospitallers in their little enclave at Borgo, and surrounded them on all sides, trapping them without any possibility of provisions reaching them from Europe or anywhere else, they would make them cave in in the end.

To the Hospitallers this became known as the Great Siege – which is one of the most illustrious exploits that fills the history pages of an Order that had to date radiated chivalrous accomplishments wherever it had set foot – again if historians who often turn out to be biased history writers of the very same Order and the only sources of information about the matter, are to be believed.

The Order's historians give the impression that all this was done in the name of Christianity and to defend the values of Christian Europe from the onslaughts of Moslem Turkey and were it not for the stand taken at Malta and Lepanto by the Christian rulers, Christianity as such would have been wiped out from Europe.

Other historians, equally validly, assert that what both these two Mediterranean super-powers were bent on was to eliminate the enemy – in order to have total and complete hegemony of a very profitable and essential trade route, the most lucrative in the then known world. The fact that one side happened to be Christian and the other Moslem was immaterial: neither did what they did moved solely by strictly religious principles.

The true history of this period may yet have to be written.

Be that as it may, the Turks were attracted to Malta because the Knights Hospitallers had made Malta their headquarters and the Maltese population as a country became involved in the Great Siege – if nothing else because of the hardship this naval embargo brought about. Not necessarily, as some historians carried away by unjustified zeal, assert in the sense that the Maltese stood four-square in defence of the (Catholic) Faith.

The majestic Conventual Church in the "New City" of Valletta manifests the order's affluence

Most Maltese did not know what was happening except that food-supplies ran low to nil during the siege. And few of them had been allowed to come anywhere near the Noble Knights of Europe – except perhaps as servants to take care of the horse-stables or as aides to help knights with their armour or as oarsmen for their galleys. Or as couriers, clandestinely carrying messages by swimming across the harbour from the Borgo battlements to the harbour fort of St Elmo. (Legendary heroic sagas about such exploits abound in Maltese epic poetry). But much of this talk about the vital Maltese contribution to the success of the defence of Malta during the Great Siege is just that.

The Knights were a self-contained war-machine and the poetical fancy of pitting Maltese warriors valiantly fighting side-by-side with Knights to fend off the infidel in defence of the Catholic Faith is quite removed from historical reality.

The Great Siege which lasted quite a few months put a strain on Malta and its resources – for the country which always had to import most of its grain, and most everything else, from Europe now found its granaries running empty. At one point the look-out fort at the entrance to the harbour, Fort St Elmo battered and ruined, had fallen to the Turks. In a barrage of cannon blasts from the strategic hill known as Monte Sciberras (today's Valletta) opposite the very Hospitallers' headquarters at Fort St Angelo, the Turks pounded the battlements and the bastions of the Knights. Resistance had come to a crisis point.

When all seemed lost and defeat seemed imminent, miraculously, on September 8th 1565 the siege was lifted and the Knights were saved an ignominious defeat. The Turks were repulsed and the Grand Master Jean Parisot de la Vallette, hailing from the Langue of France, a master strategist in the art of war and an unfailing inspiration to his fighting men, won the day.

The Order was relieved and Christian Europe temporarily saved being run over by the infidel as happened in Hungary, the

Carpathians and the Balkans. However, the Knights, ever obsessed with the reality of another attack, set about re-building their fortifications – a commitment that was to dictate the Hospitaller Order's philosophy, thinking and outlook throughout its nearly three centuries' sojourn in Malta and was to turn Malta into a bastion-fortress, physically and psychologically.

The move to Monte Sciberras

For a start, it was soon realized after the siege that a more defensible location than Borgo was needed, and eventually, the Grand Council decided to move the Order's headquarters to a safer site. In a move smacking of defiance they chose the very hill known as Monte Sciberras opposite Borgo, that very hill from which the Turks had pounded the Hospitaller positions during the Great Siege.

Once the decision was taken, the Order spent no pains or effort. The City of Valletta would be the new seat of power for the Order and it would be planned in right royal manner with a Magisterial Palace, ample spacious *auberges* for the different langues each with their respective Churches and chapels where ethnic services could be held each in their own language, as well as a common Convent Church – where the whole Order could gather for common worship or special occasions like the election of a Grand Master. Thus came to be built the Conventual Church dedicated to the Patron Saint of the Order, John the Baptist.

But above all, this New City of Valletta would be impregnable. And so the best architects of Europe were called into service and the best masons and master-builders forced into the effort. The best brains abetted by the best labour force that slave-labour could provide soon saw the City rise from the undulating depths of its own rocky substance. For the architects used the very stone that was quarried from on-site for the construction of the buildings they erected, thereby providing at the same time the labyrinthine underground maze of escape-routes and courier passages, the fresh-

The Grand Master's Palace exuded opulence, as befitted an eminent prince and ruler

Above and below: Ornate Flemish tapestries adorned the Conventual Church

water wells and the warehouses to store munitions and stable the horses below ground as the buildings went up above ground.

As a result, Valletta, built in the late 1500's, is the first city in the modern era to be planned and built in the practical grid-iron profile: from his magisterial palace, the Grand Master could keep an eye on his oftentimes rumbustious and turbulent brood. And in spite of successive predators who pillaged and raped and plundered and carried mementos away, this palace still boasts of treasures on which nobody can put a price tag. The visitor to Valletta till today marvels at the architecture of the place: one can view the sea on either side and ahead from practically any street of the City.

The Hospitallers wanted to make this city which they dubbed *Civitas Humillima* (Most Humble City) truly the most noble city of Europe, a masterpiece of their architectural tastes and a show-piece to the rest of the world – and they spared no effort in the process. Tapestries from the best tapestry-makers of Europe, the Flemish, would adorn in lavish profusion palace and conventual Church. They even threw in a seat of higher learning to be known as the *Collegium Melitense* for those among their members who were so bent. To run it they brought none other than the Jesuit Fathers, appealing directly to the founder of this new Order, to St Ignatius himself. And their request would accept no answer in the negative.

The Aftermath: Two Centuries-Plus of Hospitaller Presence

The Great Siege with the glorious military prowess shown by defensive and offensive Hospitaller strategies was to remain indelibly in the minds of many Hospitallers as the zenith of their glory, the landmark from which all other activities in their long and glorious existence would be judged.

Another landmark was their move to the new headquarters in Monte Sciberras which now took the name of Valletta, after their Great Siege hero who happened to be the Grand Master at the time, Jean Parisot de la Vallette. The Hospitallers settled in the Grand

Harbour area to a routine of bastion-building, defences-fortifying and ... waiting ... for the enemy to strike: ready to deliver the mortal blow if he as much as dared approach these shores which became impregnable – with the best architects and the best minds of Europe continually planning and expanding fortifications and building bastions and erecting cavaliers.

However, the long expected big one never came. The Turks, either because of tactical weaknesses or judgemental mistakes, never dared call again at Malta. And the Knights, eventually, settled down to a routine of petty bickering among themselves and one-upmanship with the local authorities, civil and religious. Typical of life among the idle rich, they became ambitious, vane, envious and covetous especially since they were indolent aristocrats with a lot of leisure time on their hands.

As time went on and life became an easy routine of military chores abetted by the comforts of ubiquitous and easily-available slaves and servants to do one's bidding, it was inevitable that degeneration and corruption would set in.

And both the records of the Magisterial Council sessions as well as the very Acts of the Order's own Courts and the correspondence with the Popes in Rome and the Monarchs of Europe testify to a gradual yet inevitable softening of both military discipline and the requirements of religious life. Duels became a common-place means of settling disputes among them. Revelry and carousing, ordinary ways of enjoying themselves. Unbridled excesses at festivities like Carnival became the norm. Bickering over properties and bequests an accepted way of settling disputes. Clandestine and at times brazenly open affairs with the local maidens a common means of bastardizing an already mixed nation. Free-wheeling and gambling a way of settling accounts. Homosexuality a never-raise-an-eyebrow activity that was common even in the higher echelons right up to the magisterial palace where the under-age candidates to the Order's langues served first as pages in the magisterial court.

The Grand Master had a summer residence, named after the G. M. who built it, Verdala

Grand Masters took to 'sponsoring' Maltese neighbourhoods some with majestic gates as Hompesch Gate, above, in Zabbar

Throughout all this, there remained the obsession with building. When the various fortifications and bastions were completed, it was the erection of monuments for the sake of monuments and leaving one's name in stone: on aqueducts, Churches, way-side chapels, whole villages even (Città Paola). This became a fashionable past-time. As did the garnering of honours. This could be more palpably seen in the jockeying for position, especially at the onset of illness to a Grand Master (who was practically always an old man when elected anyhow) – a crucial period which turned out all too often a succumbing to the temptation of collusion and corruption.

One must not forget either the religious under-currents that were to play a big part in the undermining of the Order: new ideas from the heretical French and German quarters and more insidiously the influence of the freemason-like secret societies that created a society within this society.

All this from within.

Added to this were the constant occasions of bickering with the local Maltese supreme authority: the *Università dei grani* at the seat of Malta's government, its capital still, Mdina at this time. Valletta was pitted against Mdina in a power struggle.

One must not forget the other strand that made this a three-way struggle for power, either. For besides the Maltese Church, under the leadership of the Canons of the Mdina Cathedral Chapter, and the Knights Hospitallers in their Magisterial splendour in Valletta, (and in due time, in the sumptuous summer residences of Verdala and San Anton) there was also, as we have seen, the Holy Inquisitor – who made his presence very much felt in these islands. His residence was in Borgo and his summer-villa at Girgenti but he presumed to be above everybody else.

For many decades, indeed for whole centuries, Malta looked more like a battle-ground of ideas and ideals, finally boiling down to positioning for power, that so tarnished its Christian overlords whether Hospitaller, Church or Inquisitorial.

With intellectual, emotional and especially religious rifts of this kind where often all caution was thrown to the wind, it was not surprising that the affluent Hospitaller Order in Malta had fallen to moral depths the likes of which it had not experienced before. And with it, the whole of the power-structure in Malta, that was more keen on asserting its privileges and prerogatives than in seriously governing by solving the very real social problems of the populace.

So the inevitable, which was only waiting for the right catalyst, happened when Napoleon Buonaparte, on his way to Egypt and his Nile Campaign, stopped over in Malta with the excuse of asking for the furnishing of much-needed supplies for his men-of-war. What the Turks with their mighty fleets and armies did not succeed in doing – namely ousting the Hospitallers from their safe haven in Malta, Napoleon and the French did.

Hompesch was the reigning Grand Master at the time and before he or his knights knew what had hit the islands, he was expropriated by an avaricious Emperor from France who was as anxious to add this little archipelago to his list of conquered territories as he was to annihilate an aristocratic Order that had dared side with the Monarchy against him back in France.

It was 1798 and the Knights Hospitallers of St John of Jerusalem, the members of that Venerable Order which, because of its long association with Malta came to be known as the Knights of Malta, were to find themselves once more without a home: this time dispersed throughout Europe and eventually suffering the plight of neglect. As the Templars, at least those of them who might have survived the merciless decimation and slaughter of their members back in France, would have said: History has a way of repeating itself for as you do, so it will be done unto you!

Chapter 10

The Age of French Duplicity

(1798 – 1800)

Napoleon's utter hostility for the monarchy and the aristocracy was notorious. As such he had little tolerance for the Knights Hospitallers of St John of Jerusalem who hailed from all the noblest and best aristocratic families of Europe. To add to all this was the fact that the French peninsula was represented in Malta by three *langues:* Provence, Auvergne and France, which latter at the time was a state within what we know today as the nation of France. Some of these Hospitallers had taken sides with the traditional monarchy and against the liberating Napoleonic revolution. But the provenance of these French-leaning members of the Order in Malta is important for another reason: some of them might have been instrumental in making Napoleon's arrival here less unwelcome than it could have otherwise been.

Already during the French Revolution in 1792, the revolutionaries had shown their low regard for the aristocracy by confiscating the Commanderies of these three langues and declaring the Order of St John to be dissolved and non-exisent there.

However, there were other types of French connections in Malta that must have contributed to making Napoleon's take-over of the islands easier than he had imagined. For a start there was a strong Masonic presence here – which had started earlier under the

Hospitallers, mostly with members hailing precisely from the countries of the French peninsula. After all freemasonry was very strong in France because it had found political asylum and spiritual refuge there.

Historians theorize that, after the squelching of the Knights Templars by papal fiat in the whole of Europe back in the fourteenth century, most such ex-Templars had gone underground and survived in France. Hence in that country there must have existed a strong tie with the surviving Templars. The Templars, it must be remembered had originated contemporaneously with the Hospitallers and the Teutonic knights back in the Holy Land at the time of the Crusades. The Templars, as we have seen, took their name from their title which originally read: Knights of the Holy Sepulchre which is *the* Temple, hence Templars.

Their *raison d'etre,* even as manifested in their symbols, had been as a building society. They constructed impregnable fortresses, majestic buildings and sumptuous palaces. They had been known for their building abilities or masonry and now, underground, they had become *free* masons – released of their vows because they were ordered disbanded by a papal decree, but not of their comradeship and sense of fraternity. Even though, for fear of persecution and being burnt at the stake as heretics, they could not profess themselves publicly, they could still band together clandestinely. Hence the reason for their secrecy.

These surviving Templars – now become underground free-masons – also had a score to settle with the Hospitallers. It was after all at the instigation of the Hospitallers that the Pope had been persuaded to suppress the Order of the Knights Templars. And the Hospitallers had suddenly become wealthy by inheriting much of the Templars' possessions, commanderies, bailiwicks, priories and uncountable other pieces of real estate and mobile assets.

Hence the presence of the freemasons in Malta – which has been historically established as having strong roots already at the beginning of the 1700's – was very threatening to the State and the Church: the reason why the Knights and Grand Masters as well as Holy Inquisitors spared no effort to expel away from the islands anyone they suspected of masonry here. However, the Authorities had a hard time identifying them and bringing them to trial even though there is reason to believe they incubated within the Order itself. Which shows, in a way, that the Order was not as compact as it should have been: there were some subversive elements within it holding clandestine meetings, fomenting discontent who went undetected – or at least were indulgently tolerated. Another indication perhaps of the lax state of affairs to which the Order had degenerated.

Added to this was the fact that the local populace for one reason or another – mostly because of the high-handed way the haughty Knights had begun to deal with the Maltese – began harbouring resentment at this foreign power that kept aloof, kept to itself and looked disdainfully on them. The Leaders of the people, that is the local *Università* (the ruling body of nobles) based in Mdina could not stomach that they were never consulted in things that mattered about the local government of their own country, especially when it came to taxes and tax-collecting. They saw the Knights ever more and more as arrogant intruders – of whom they could not wait to be rid. And the opportunity, when it would present itself from whatever quarter, was not to be missed.

It was in this overall picture of the local scene, all of which could be of help and assistance to any foreign power with an eye to invading the country, that Napoleon stopped over in Malta. And Napoleon had an eye on invading the world. He was on his way to the Nile, in fact, as part of his Egyptian Campaign when he stopped in Malta purportedly to supply his fleet with much needed supplies.

The Grand Master at the time was a German, Ferdinand von Hompesch and when confronted with this quandary, he realized that should he refuse, Napoleon would storm Malta and take what

The solid silver gates of the Blessed Sacrament Chapel of St John's were saved from French greed by being painted black

he wanted anyhow. Should he accede to his request, it was like letting in the wolf into one's fold! So he did the next best thing: he negotiated how this could be done with the least possible embarassment to the Order and the least shedding of blood. He offered no resistance. In fact, it is said that due to the many French sympathizers within the fortified places, the actual defence was never as effective as it should have been.

The city that had spent centuries and tons of gold and silver in expensive and formidable fortifications, was now bereft of any power to resist.

Weighted down as the Order in Malta was with luxury and licentiousness, the absence of real work, the possession of great wealth that softened the military discipline and soldierly vigilance, it was inevitable that this should be so. The intruder could walk in and walk all over. The Order of the Knights Hospitallers of St John of Jerusalem that had so bravely withstood the onslaught of Turk and corsair throughout its history, could not resist the enemy within: sloth brought about by affluence.

The Knights were in disgrace and completely ruined. They left Malta to disperse to the countries of their origin or wherever they were given sanctuary. Many fled to Russia where they received a hearty welcome from the Czar Paul I who declared himself Protector of the Order – especially since thereby he was defying Napoleon Buonaparte, that commoner-presuming-to-royalty, that supreme anarchist who did not respect the aristocracy, still less the monarchy.

The French in Malta

The French soon set about establishing themselves. However, very soon even the French sympathizers among the Maltese realized that no sooner had one type of tyrant left these shores than another one, a more ruthless one, took its place: the Hospitallers were superseded by Napoleon. By and large, the French did not leave a happy legacy in Malta. Anxious to eradicate all traces of Hospitaller presence, they set about demolishing and pillaging and raping the palaces, the convents, the Churches, the baronial mansions and the stately homes. In fact they carried away anything they could plunder. They also tried to impose or rather super-impose their own mode of government which put a Frenchman in charge of any key position or location in Malta – especially one where tangible, material lucre was to be had.

The people of course, resented this. Even those franco-philes, of whom there were many in Malta, who had believed that the French presence might make a difference because it would be more humane than the Hospitaller form of government were sadly disappointed.

Having established his Lieutenant to take care of business locally, Napoleon and his fleet proceeded to the Nile – with much of Malta's loot on board. There the French suffered a rousing defeat at the hands of the British at the mouth of the Nile and much of what Napoleon had stolen from Malta must be lying under layers of sediment down in the River Nile. Other precious material found its way to public and private collections. In the Louvre there is the sword presented to Grand Master Jean Parisot de La Vallette by King Philip II of Spain which is on exhibit in the French Museum as a *gift* from Malta when actually it was part of the loot stolen from these islands.

As far as the relationship of the Maltese with the French was concerned, it was inevitable that discontent with the New Occupiers of the island who were more arrogant still – if that were possible – than their previous despots would begin to rub people the wrong way.

Word spread among the populace, especially by means of the members of the *Dejma* – which as we have seen earlier was a sort of reserve defence force that the Maltese had set up centuries before to band together in case of emergencies from corsairs and pirates. By bringing together all the village people of a particular area anytime danger was sighted, the village leader could mobilize whatever forces were necessary in terms of personnel as well as equipment, arms or ammunition to ward off the enemy. Now, during the French occupation, this system which had been originally set up to defend the islands against the foreign enemy, found itself defending Malta from the enemy within.

It was this network, about whose existence the haughty French knew little and could understand still less because they were not told about it, that eventually galvanized the local peasants and at a pre-agreed sign (the pealing of Church-bells of the Carmelite Church at Mdina), the peasantry brandishing anything they could lay their hands on besides rakes and shovels, marched on Mdina and like a puny yet courageous David took on this foreign Goliath. Eventually the rebellion, fanned mostly by the degree of discontent among a people made desperate and with nothing to lose, spread to other towns and villages of Malta and Gozo.

The French tried to defend themselves by locking themselves up in the fortifications. But these proved their own undoing, for the Maltese on the outside knew all the tricks on the inside. Besides, by locking themselves in, the French would last as long as their supplies would last for the people outside controlled what went in. They could wait as long as was needed. And soon enough the French realized that they were beaten by the hardy locals.

As Destiny would have it, Lord Horatio Nelson happened to be hovering around the Mediterranean around these times and this must definitely have tilted the balance and started a new era – the Anglo-Maltese love affair with all its ups and downs.

Ironically the French Revolution which purported to give more power to the people as the famous slogan: **Fraternitè, Egalitè, Libertè** avers, manifested none of these high-sounding principles at all in Malta. The common people here definitely gained little if anything at all from the French presence. The fact that the heroes of this uprising against the French were common peasants and common folk adds more mockery still to the whole presence of the

The French tried to erase Hospitaller landmarks in Malta – even unto defacing Hospitaller coat-of-arms on buildings

Dun Mikiel Xerri is considered a patriotic priest who stood up to French tyranny. He and his companions were shot to death

French in Malta about which the less said the better. Not so the native heroes who are honoured as true liberators by the Maltese. And so, another despot, a hated one this time, that ruled Malta with an iron fist, bit the dust and was made to depart in a short-lived stay of less than two years.

Meantime they left behind them some unenviable bequests: memories of atrocities perpetrated by the likes of General Vaubois and Francois Masson and the many Maltese heroes who were shot to death for plotting to overthrow the hated regime among whom we find Dun Mikiel Xerri.

Chapter 11

The Age of British Colonialism

(1800–1964)

In a span of two years, the Maltese Islands saw the departure of two sets of overlords: one was known as the Knights Hospitallers of St John of Jerusalem and the other was the newly-formed revolutionary force of Napoleon's France.

Now, in 1800, came the British – supposedly because the people of Malta requested their help and supposedly also for the local population's own good. Actually there was a very strong reason why the Maltese asked for British protection: the British were a very mighty naval power at the time and they were also in the process of building that empire over which the sun would never set.

When one thinks that this tiny nation called England had extended its influence, control and power over most of the nations that counted in the world, from the Indies in the East to the Carribean in the West, on to Hawaii and Australia, one can begin to grasp the magnitude and the magnificence of the British Empire; an empire based on the good old-fashioned principles that *might is right*. And might in those times meant a powerful fleet manned with patriotic and/or mercenary sailors backed by patriotic and/or mercenary soldiers ready to serve and die for God, king and country and filthy lucre – all items practically always interchangeable. Reward enough to be given a share of the booty in the shape of a lucrative post in the far-flung empire once in a deserving while.

Hence, the more outposts were won, the more loyal administrators were needed – even though, most often the requirement for such positions were the colour of the British skin and the sound of the English accent and the loyalty to the British crown without too much attention being given to any particular proficiency the job at hand required. And so, these outposts of the far-flung empire, very much in the steps and methods of the old Roman Empire after all and every empire since, became 'little Englands' around the world bound together by a common language, a common law, a uniform mode of government with loyal administrators more often than competent ones. And, often, united by a common – Anglican – religion.

So in 1800, Malta was to become another colony in the long chain of *little Englands* around the globe.

True, Malta did not offer much by way of natural resources. But it did by way of booty. And strategic position.

Situated as it is astride the Mediterranean, half-way between North Africa and Europe and again mid-way between Egypt and Gibraltar, Malta could be the ideal stop-off place for this Mediterranean sea-route especially since its naturally protected harbours were ideal sheltering-places from Mediterranean winds and storms. All this was sterling stuff indeed for an Empire that depended on its fleet for its very survival when naval mobility and fire-power counted above all else. And where control of the Mediterranean could be a deterrent to any budding or ambitious *big power* of the Teutonic, Russian or French kind. This was more truly so when the opening of the Suez Canal – de Lesseps' architectural masterpiece – meant that the Mediterranean achieved a new and compelling role, a short cut in the Britain-Far East (India) route.

So what more welcome excuse than this could Nelson have to come to terms with the Maltese by offering them protection against the enemy – whoever and wherever that may be or come from? And

Queen Adelaide's burning desire was to see an Anglican church built in Malta
– symbolically on the site of the German langue

offer protection he and the British Empire did, by supplanting whatever had gone before and, in keeping with the colonial policy of the time, imposing the British way of doing things.

It took some time for all the details to be worked out, but with powerful allies one can achieve a lot in a short time. By the Treaty of Paris (in 1814) Malta was well and truly placed under the protection of the British Crown. Henceforward, under British Rule, Malta would have the local Representative of the Monarch, a Governor. Naturally, he would be British. To help him govern, he would have around him a group of reliable and trustworthy men, naturally also British. These would in turn need a number of advisers to help them execute the defence plans, architectural masterpieces, essential-services projects (like water and sewage), educational reforms, criminal justice, etc., that the Islands might need. Naturally all these would be British.

Primarily, all this administration, facilitating and protection would be geared for those people specifically living in the *safe enclaves* spread all over the islands – who all happened to be British. Little if anything would be done for the *natives*, for these were not the main concern of the colonialists – except in a spill-over effect sort of way.

Even the currency was, naturally, British: the very same coins and paper-money as were current in England with the same icon of the same Monarch on the obverse and some British monument or royal coat-of-arms on the reverse.

In a policy that was geared to pass on the civilizing influence of British ideals on to the colony, it was essential for the survival of.the integrity of the ideals of the Empire that the Upper Crust and the Upper Echelons would hail from the Mother Country. A water-tight caste system would tolerate the colonized locals as servants of the Crown in the humbler capacities as clerks, couriers, messengers, go-fers on land, or at sea as non-commissioned officers, as ordinary seamen in the many British navy and commercial ships as well as in the vitally important yards that built or repaired ships.

The *natives* gladly participated at this level for somehow, no matter how low or humble the capacity in which one served, one shared in the might of the Empire itself. Or at least, so was one made to believe by a domineering presence ever anxious to foster the smooth running of affairs by making sure of subservience from a grateful populace. Thus it was an unwritten (or maybe written) law of colonial policy that the local people, no matter how qualified (and not too many were allowed to be too qualified), could never be allowed to achieve a rank beyond a certain level of grateful subservience.

To start with, education was re-shuffled so that by the mid-19th century, schooling, what little there was of it for those who could afford it, had to be done in English. The justice system super-imposed a lot of British jurisprudence on what was already a legal hotch-potch of feudalism, Hospitaller wisdom and French bonapartist legal principles. From the regal aristocracy of the Knights, to the pronounced republicanism of the French, Malta now passed to the adulation of the Monarchy.

As such, Malta, a country that for all practical purposes was part and parcel of the far-flung British Empire on which the sun never set, would receive the visits of British Royalty which would become occasions of much celebration among the British population as well as the loyal local populace – if they could ever bring themselves to fully understand what the fuss was all about.

This was indeed the core of the colonial policy of England, the main reason for the setting up and buttressing of a Colonial Office and the key to British colonial success: the colonized nations were conditioned to believe that being under the Union Jack was a sign of providential predilection; accepting the foreign rulers a sign of civilized behaviour; bowing to the foreign form of government, foreign language, foreign justice-system – even foreign idiosyncracies – a way of showing gratitude.

True, possessing a British passport opened up international frontiers that hitherto had been brick-wall barriers. One could go

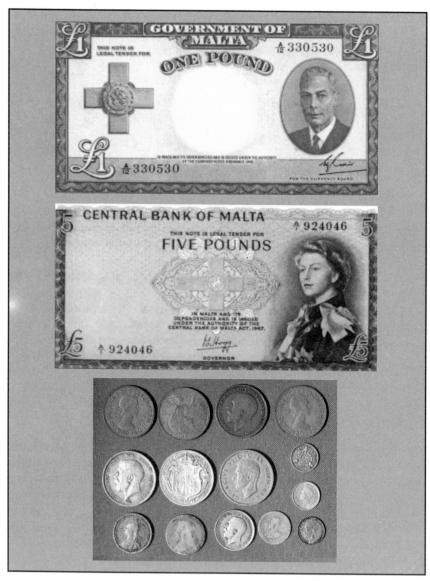

Malta's paper money and coins (as well as the stamps) bore the image of the reigning British monarch

The famous "Victoria Lines" – that were built to provide defence from attack by sea

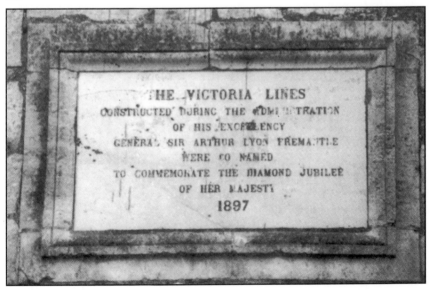

anywhere in the world – literally to the ends of the earth – where the British Empire extended and beyond, and still feel at home; even though as a colonized person you could not really settle in England or be made welcome there: foreigners and colonials alike were politely tolerated in the Mother Country only for purposes of *further training* which very often meant further conditioning in things British – and then back to one's own mother-country it was to further abet the colonial policy in one's own fatherland.

All of this subtle but steadfast indoctrination was inculcated in a colonial school system that projected England as the pinnacle of civilization and being British the culmination of being human.

The Maltese islands were no exception. From now on, everything in Malta became the property of His or Her Majesty's Government: land, sea, sky, ships, ministries, buildings, gardens, offices and paper-clips.

This, by and large, was the system adopted in Malta during the stay of the British on the islands of Malta and Gozo. It may not have been all delivered at one go: but over the years, it became a policy that was more systematic and more pronounced. And in a way, once the Maltese woke up to reality, they realized that this system was not any different from that of the arrogant French before them and the haughty Hospitallers before that.

The benefits from British Rule

In their 160-odd years here, of course, the British did a lot for Malta. Or rather Malta happened to be the beneficiary because the British were here. For one thing, being the sea-base that it is, Malta was an important stop-over place in this maritime route especially, as has been mentioned, with the inauguration of the new sea-lanes made possible by the opening of the Suez Canal. But this very strategic position in the Mediterranean also saw Malta involved in many wars, simply because Malta happened to be associated with Britain, as a colony of that country.

The Crimean War saw a number of wounded soldiers and refugees taken care of in the islands. The First World War as well. The Maltese, as British subjects/citizens could also join the British Forces or those allied with Britain – to serve in certain humble ranks. Both the Crimean War and the First World War brought home to the authorities concerned, among other things, that the practice of medicine in Malta was in a sorry state. Rather ironical – since nursing and taking care of the sick and administering hospitals was the primary vocation of the Knights Hospitallers of St John of Jerusalem. But now the authorities realized that beyond the *Sacra Infermeria*, their main hospital in Valletta which catered mostly for the sick and infirm patients of the Order itself even unto serving them in silver cutlery and dishes, the Order had done little for the health and the sanitary well-being of the populace at large beyond establishing poor houses and old people's homes.

In fact, outbreaks of plagues bubonic and otherwise, were quite common. In popular credence, recourse to miraculous intervention of the saints (especially St Roque, the specific protector of the plague-stricken) was a substitute for sensible health care.

Now it was the turn of the British to build hospitals all over the islands but they were there to cater for their own sick more than for the health and well-being of the local people. These latter were kept at a safe distance. The appalling conditions of everyday existence in Malta was a constant struggle for survival with sewage and drinking-water being primary health hazards. And in an age when medicine was preoccupied with curative rather than preventive measures, doctors were kept very busy indeed.

But what has indelibly linked Malta's fate with that of Britain was surely that nefarious Nazi-masterminded piece of evil depravity.

The Second World War

Malta, as a fully-fledged British colony and hence a proven ally of the West, found herself embroiled in another war, the Second World

Replica of a World War II plane: 3 such comprised Malta's air defence. A disused shelter – happily fallen on bad times

War. For the incurable romantics of the world of martial arts, Malta's contribution to this conflagration is seen as a sign of solidarity with the West, or rather with the Allies, against the forces of evil, the Axis. However, as has been mentioned already, Malta had inalienable and traditional ties of the linguistic, cultural, historical and geographical kind with the European continent and especially with Italy more than with far-away England. And in Malta during the war there were many sympathizers who sided with the Italians and even with Mussolini.

So it is to be expected that there was a segment of the Maltese nation that sympathized with the Axis Cause (Italian-German) and so professed publicly. In fact to the British, such as these showed subversive sympathies against the Empire by siding with the enemies of the British Empire. For their loyalty to the enemy, such citizens were exiled, interned in concentration camps for the duration of the war in British Africa where tempers could cool off and more sensible outlooks prevail. And among these exiles were to be found such patriots as Neriku Mizzi, Herbert Ganado and a host of others who would eventually become the leaders of the secession movement from Britain – at any cost even at that of merging with near-by Italy.

But by and large, the population dug in its heels and pulled together with the Allies, probably because it had little choice anyhow. It was made to believe that this was for its own good – it being their own good fortune to be on the side of the Forces of Good against the Forces of Evil. Again, because of its geographical destiny in the middle of the Mediterranean, Malta had to be brought to heel for in the Axis blue-print for the conquest of North Africa, Malta, within sixty miles of Sicily, would be the logical supply base. Except that Malta, as a British base, stood in the way and therefore had to be eliminated.

Or conquered.

By a constant barrage of bombs and explosions on the island that went on, sometimes non-stop, for months on end, the native population was often reduced to the condition of rats burrowing in underground shelters for protection to avoid the blitzkrieg. And scrounging around for whatever was edible on land or sea when food supplies ran out during the protracted siege.

To add to the misery, the carpet bombing also hit at the convoys sent by Britain to Malta carrying much-needed supplies of ammunition but also of food for a starved populace and, in certain times of desperate destitution, even of drinking water of which Malta had run out.

Many a time Malta was on the brink of surrender and giving up the ghost. But every time, with the might of the British Forces to help push the miracle, Malta survived the disaster. The heavy losses in terms of planes, boats, ships, buildings but above all human lives were catastrophic. And neither Malta nor Britain want to forget those days of cataclysm when the world seemed to come to an end.

The miraculous entry into Grand Harbour of a crippled and depleted convoy of ships that brought much-needed supplies in basic food commodities and essential ammunition for the defence positions on August 15th 1942 – the convoy known as the *Santa Marija* – is still vividly engraved in the memory of the war generation, and recalled by a nation that back then was often on the verge of raising the white flag. The fact that it happened on the Feast of the Assumption of Mary, a feast dear to many Maltese, gave it a religious significance to a believing nation that boosted morale and electrified people to resist some more. The heroics of these war years are remembered on many fronts: books, audio and visual presentations, drama and many other ways. The untold sacrifices and uncounted dead – both civilians and servicemen – that this war brought in its wake is still vivid in the memories of the older generation.

As a result of her gallantry during the War and its resistance to the enemy, Malta as a nation was awarded the George Cross by none other than His Majesty George VI of England – a symbol that became embedded in the very red-and-white flag of Malta and has remained

Convoys of food, but more often stricken ships, limped into Malta's harbour

The George Cross on exhibit in St George's Square (now Palace Square). Even though Valletta was in ruins, this award was a great boost to national morale

there ever since. There would come a time, though, (blasphemously so for the local anglo-philes) like the pre-Independence era, when anti-British sentiments among certain sections of the populace ran so high that the chant was heard: *We cannot eat the George Cross* – signifying thereby that the Maltese would rather have equitable justice done to them in terms of jobs and fair deals than have honours heaped upon them – honours which could not be translated into much-needed food. But that was to come later on. Right now in the immediate post-war years, Malta's fight was for survival.

Post-War Malta

Immediately following the war, the situation in Malta was very precarious: the suspension of schooling and still more higher learning, during the war years made of Malta and the Maltese a nation barely managing to survive, inured to hardship and strangers to luxury. This situation also brought about a lack of employment opportunities – barring such as were open only to unskilled labourers and the occasional or seasonal unsteady work, mostly related to jobs required by the British Services in Malta.

With an ever-increasing because ever faithfully Catholic population, and so many mouths to feed in a country without too many natural resources, poverty and starvation were staring the population in the face, even in the post-war years of peace.

It being the policy of the then government not to solve the poverty issue by creating jobs or raising the standard of living, the easy solution at hand was for the British Government in Malta to shift people around: emigration.

And so a massive exodus began in the 40's right after the war – mostly towards Australia, but also to Canada. A number of Maltese, also, who had settled in the United States earlier in the century, seeing the plight of their fellow-countrymen, began 'sponsoring' over some of their relatives to settle in North America.

As to emigration of the Maltese towards Australia: it is an intriguing phenomenon that went on through the 40's and 50's and 60's and that saw hundreds of thousands of Maltese leave their homeland in what often were nothing but cattle-ships, to settle in that far-away continent under what became known as the 'assisted passages' scheme. The hosting government needed labour desperately and was ready to pay most of the expenses for the trip to entice labourers for its cane-fields, in return for a guaranteed minimum two years' pay-back in work in the new homeland.

Many Maltese took the opportunity to make a go of it Down Under. A great number went there and stayed, setting up home and settling for good. A number of others, missing the close family ties that exist in a small island like Malta and feeling lost in a big continent like Australia, preferred to head back home at the first opportunity. Even though they had to pay some penalties, including their fare back to the Australian government since they had come back to Malta before the two-year contract date. Home-sickness took its toll because for many it was the first time they were away from their families and their homes for any length of time.

For the settlers went in waves: first went the husband who would try to find a steady job, try to find lodging and try to settle down in this new land and this new and sometimes hostile environment. Once the head of the family was established, he would sponsor over the rest of the family: the wife and children and sometimes in-laws, in the case of married children.

Under the best of circumstances, this was a monstrous arrangement. With the Maltese – who are perhaps more attached to their families and home-land than most – it was deadly.

Many just turned around and came back. Others tried it out for a time and could not stick it. Especially since most of the work available was cutting sugar-cane in the immense plantations – to many a new form of slave-labour, for whites. Indeed the story of the hardship that the Maltese immigrants to Australia encountered has still to be written for even here many suffered discrimination because they were from the southern reaches of the Mediterranean and hence, in racist discriminatory circles, not thoroughbred white Europeans. Besides there was a language barrier: what little English these ordinary labourers spoke, was often not Aussie English. And they could be detected a mile away. The result was that many Maltese formed their own colonies with their own kind for protection against the heavy odds if nothing else, with the consequence that immigrant ghettoes sprouted up: Maltese colonies in Australia.

In North America and Canada the story was somewhat different. It helps a lot if you have somebody you know or is related to you who sets the stage for you, as happened in these two countries. And many of these Maltese managed to sponsor over their relatives and friends.

As to immigration of Maltese into Great Britain: this country was tolerably close to Malta and those who settled there could easily come back for a visit to renew contacts with relatives and friends and to touch bases with one's roots. Besides, the British Services and the merchant navy had employed many Maltese personnel who found themselves equally at home in Britain as in Malta.

Thus, a nation that had always been at the cross-roads of history, with a sea-faring tradition and one that looked outwards away from its shores, was now forced to do it by dint of absolute exigency: survival in this over-crowded nation depended on settling abroad, finding a job elsewhere and striking roots in a foreign land. Being a nation-member of the British Empire (and later the British Commonwealth) and thus owning a British passport helped considerably in all this. And this much worked in favour of the Maltese settling abroad. More than that, though, it was the hard-working gutsy tenacity to make good and show-them-back-home-that-we-have-done-well-for-ourselves-in-spite-of-the-heavy-odds that kept many of the Maltese going.

And so this tiny dot in the Mediterranean, which must rank

with Gibraltar as one of the most lilliputian of British possessions, would now be all set to export to the rest of the world its most prized possession: its people. A job-scarcity situation that brought the spectres of the fear of famine and poverty back home was a strong enough sociological factor.

However, exporting your people is hardly the best way to reconstruct a nation especially after a war that had bled you to death. But, as we shall see, even this ordeal helped launch Malta into the modern era in the modern world.

A precious British bequest

Among the more important bequests that the British presence left in Malta must surely be counted the parliamentary form of government. Of course this did not happen overnight. In fact, at first it was the Governor (always British) and his entourage (always British), in true colonial fashion, that ruled the islands, with the locals allowed some *derivative and restricted* authority on the local village level. And things went on their merry way like this for ages. It took decades, many decades but eventually things had to change. At first slowly and imperceptibly, then more strongly, things began to change: especially as the Maltese sent for further studies in England returned home and saw the difference between the parliamentary way things were run in England and the autocratic way they were run in Malta. The Maltese began to demand and to be condescendingly allowed to take part in the political processes that concerned them. By the 1940's there was even some promise of self-government.

The full history of the intrigue, ploys and counter-ploys, Colonial Office promises made and broken, betrayals and disappointments and such stuff of which the political life, especially that of a colony, is made, has still to be written. However, the slow easing into a democratic form of government was being assured – albeit, perhaps, unconsciously. After all the Maltese had the

Eversince the Knights – who planned its grid-iron symmetry, Valletta has remained the capital and the heart of Malta

opportunity to observe the best trainers of all, those schooled in the seat of the Mother of Parliaments. Not that the British were too anxious to let the Maltese in on the secret of their own governance. As we have seen, they were kept at a certain level of civil service grades beyond which they could not go. And the same happened in the Armed Forces. In a Catch-22 sort of bind, they could not go beyond certain grades because they were considered intellectually and politically incapable and yet they needed a certain political and bureaucratic experience to come to the level of self-governing.

However, there came a time when Malta and the Maltese began to assert themselves and after a number of tentative attempts at elections (guided and monitored by those who knew better), the Maltese realized that the time had come for them to run their own country without outside interference. That the transition was made in the most civilized manner possible, without bloodshed and aggression, is in itself to the credit of all concerned. That the Maltese learned to run their country, complete with elections – run on proportional representation and all – has helped immeasurably to see Malta ease into the twentieth century in what can be considered a civilized democratic sort of way.

There is no doubt that the political and parliamentary system in Malta has the British stamp all over it. And it has stood the country in good stead as it moved into the post-Independence modern era to take its place among the family of nations.

Chapter 12

The Age of Independence and Freedom

(1964 and 1979)

For a number of decades, in fact for a century and a half, things proceeded their merry way under British rule in Malta. However, there were rumblings that began to be heard and that eventually culminated in what came to be regarded as the peaceful acquisition of independence of the Maltese Islands and Maltese people from Britain. The process takes some patient re-tracing.

For centuries, the majority of the people, kept at the basic level of survival, had little leisure to enjoy the finer things of life. They also had little time, mercifully, for reflection on their sorry plight as a colonized people. However, the very few that did, began to question the state of things. And their conclusion was that the state of the nation or rather the colony of Malta under the British was very convoluted indeed.

For one thing, there had always existed a strong pro-Italian community in Malta whose sympathies lay with the language of Dante as well as with the descendants of Romulus and Remus as a nation. The segment of the nation with this strong Italian sentiment was further abetted with the arrival in Malta of Italian refugees fleeing the repercussions of the upheavals concomitant with the vicissitudes of the various wars and movements in the peninsula: Garibaldi is said to have sought asylum in Malta and so did Pius IX, though on different occasions and for different reasons – and not together.

However, this periodic influx of outsiders, opened up the educated Maltese upper-class who had long affected an Italian mode of living besides using Italian as their means of communication.

Such pin-pricks at the Empire did not sit well with the British who would have preferred a more homogeneous, therefore more controllable population. Opening up linguistic frontiers also opened up mental ones and the reformist mentality that was sweeping over certain parts of Europe could not help have some impact on the Maltese intelligentsia (what little there was of it in the shape of lawyers and doctors and clergymen) if no one else.

Another pro-foreign faction in Malta had strong ties with the French language, culture, literature and mode of living. In spite of the bad taste that the French two-year presence on the islands had left in the hearts and minds of many in Malta, there were still those who had taken to the French and who had even migrated to that land of free speech and liberal *Illuminèe* thinking. All this necessarily meant that such as these were unsympathetic to the British presence in Malta and, unkindest cut of all, held the *Marseillaise* in higher esteem than the *God Save*.

To add to all this convoluted melting-pot, there were the various handfuls of promising and deserving Maltese intellectuals who had been rewarded by the British Administration with stints of further civilizing studies in the Mother Country. Besides being re-inforced in the belief of the supremacy of the British way of life as they gratefully applied themselves to their particular fields of study back in England, such individuals could not help noticing that over there, there was such a thing called Parliament. In fact, England boasted of being the country where true parliamentary procedure first saw the light of history. These Maltese in England also noticed that Parliament there had a bigger say in the running of the country's affairs than anything the Maltese as a nation had back in Malta.

The Road to Statehood

And so, the movement sprouted that began demanding at minimum a presence of Maltese representation on any governing bodies that took decisions relating to Malta and the Maltese. To date all such decisions had been taken by foreigners, i.e the British overlords without any Maltese involvement at all.

These ideas gathered momentum and the movement grew into a national chorus.

There were people like Lord Strickland, others like Manwel Dimech whose actions and ideas went some length in paving the way for independent thinking.

As to Lord Strickland who was born in Malta: he made quite an impact on the local scene. In fact he even founded a political party and as its leader was even Prime Minister of Malta for a time. But his influence was not limited to politics. His party was put under an interdict by the Catholic Church which became a mill-stone around his neck, and a mile-stone in Maltese history – at least as far as religious emancipation is concerned.

An ecclesiastical interdict, at a time when the Church's influence was very strong and could dictate political trends, was a powerful weapon indeed. Such an interdict places anybody pertaining to or voting for that particular Party under automatic excommunication. This means that he/she is no longer, as a Catholic, considered able to participate in Church activities and so in general, in a society that is strongly Catholic, practically ostracized since faithful Catholics are prohibited even from associating with such individuals, and, indeed are canon-law bound to positively shun them.

The interdicted are not even given Christian burial in a hallowed ground (cemetery) where Catholics are buried, but are buried separately in non-consecrated grounds, known as the 'dung-hill'. Lord Strickland and his party and those who followed his policies suffered all accursed evils incumbent on all who tangled with Church power.

But the tentative step – defiance of authority, this time ecclesiastical – and hence a sort of emancipation and liberation, had been taken. (When this interdict business was to be repeated in the 60's, this time against anybody who voted for the Labour Party under Dom Mintoff, the expected results – of scaring the Labour-voting public from voting Labour – did not materialize, further re-inforcing the voting public's sense of liberation and maturity in voting as it saw fit; which is what true democracy is all about.)

As to Manwel Dimech: he was a native-born Maltese with outlandish (for his time) socialist ideas. But influence the thinking of some of the political leaders of Malta the ideas of Manwel Dimech did. Emancipated thinking and therefore the ability to stand up and be counted against heavy odds leaning heavily in favour of authority was the seed of independent thinking and therefore of independence.

A tentative self-government concession

In the late 1940's, after repeated dilly-dallying, some semblance of self-government was granted to the Maltese – but such autonomy always carried the proviso that the resident British Governor would have to give final sanction and approval of any and all legislative decisions arrived at on the local level and that had any bearing at all on national and international policy. Still a very limiting proviso – and very far from a parliamentary democracy, hence not fully acceptable to those among the local leaders who wanted more power to the people, the local people, i.e. the Maltese.

Even then the idea of this limited concession of power was very parsimoniously made: over a long period of time, indeed decades, limited self-government was the only concession made to any semblance of local government. For it did not sit well with the local representatives of the Monarch, their Majesties' Government to grant the Maltese anything else or beyond that. Still the logic of the Malta position could not be gainsaid: one cannot vaunt oneself as

H.R.H. The Duke of Edinburgh "handing the instruments" on Malta's first Independence Day, 21st September 1964

the champion of the democratic form of government and not listen to the *demos,* i.e., the populace which in this case was Malta and its citizens who were not privy to any decisions made in their own regard but had such decisions made for them by foreigners who understood neither their culture nor their mentality or language.

The tentative half-hearted compromises made with a beast called self-government soon brought home more forcefully still to the Maltese politicians (or what budding samples there were of this uncherished breed) the fact that since, in practice, they as a parliamentary, governing body had to refer to a superior body, i.e., the Governor or H.M. Government, for the latter's approval of all of the decisions taken, there was precious little self-government except in cosmetic terms.

It took years of struggle, negotiations and delay but eventually, the infant and eccentric movement that had started in the 20's was to culminate in a patriotic chorus that achieved independence for Malta on the 21st of September of the year 1964.

So much for some semblance of political independence. However, the Maltese Islands were still dependent in a very practical manner, for their sustenance, on the foreign presence in Malta. Malta was one big military base, in essence leased to a foreign power, NATO and a foreign military presence, Great Britain. Even much of its economy was geared towards and oiled by such military alliances. And so the same chorus that clamoured for independence, went on to procure the withdrawal of all the British and foreign forces from the islands of Malta and Gozo which agreement was put into effect on the 31st of March of the year 1979.

And all this by diplomacy, bargaining, haggling and without the shedding of one drop of blood – unlike what, unfortunately, was the case with many ex-colonies of the British Empire.

Indeed, ironically, at one point in the independence negotiations, there was talk of a total and absolute integration with Britain – a desperate ploy by some local politicians to try to call British bluff

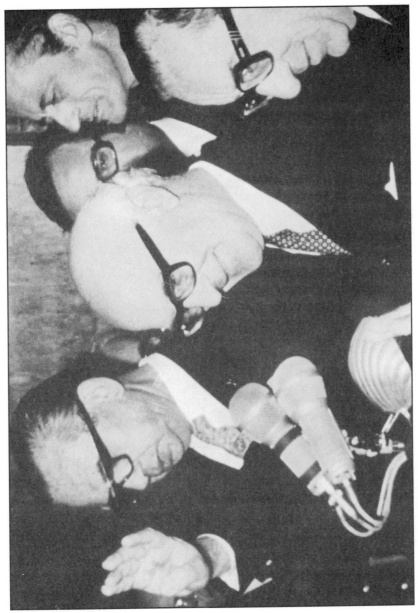

Malta was declared a Republic on 13th December 1974

31st March 1979 – The departure of H.M.S. London

The crowd at Lascaris Wharf seeing history being made – H.M.S. London leaving harbour

by demanding a voice in Westminster, thus putting Malta at least on a par with a regular electoral district in Great Britain. But this idea did not carry the day for obviously impractical reasons.

This, in the briefest of sketches, is what the Maltese achieved. But thereby hangs a tale for depending on whether one is a Labourite or a Nationalist, one will have different perspectives as to when the Modern Era for Malta began.

The Nationalists hold that it took place when their then leader Dr George Borg Olivier as Prime Minister of Malta negotiated Malta's independence from Britain which was achieved, after long and difficult manouvering, on the 21st September 1964, which day is observed by this segment of Maltese as Independence Day.

However, even after independence, counter the Labourites, Malta still retained its status as a militarily-aligned nation with its land being leased to NATO as a base. Therefore it was allied strongly with the Western powers, mostly for economic reasons since it could not definitely sever all ties with the West especially such as provided substantial revenue for such military leases. This subservience to and alignment with a foreign power, even one like NATO, was considered by the Malta Labour Party as constituting a strong economic and political dependence on a foreign power. So, in contrast to the Nationalists, the Labourites hold that true independence for Malta came when Malta, under Dom Mintoff, negotiated the withdrawal from the island (*kicked out* is the irresponsible term used at times) of all foreign troops including the British. It was only then that, having given up its military image as a naval, army or air force base, Malta emancipated itself from its war heritage and veered its economy towards other means of sustenance such as those of the industrial kind.

Thus according to the Malta Labour Party, it was only on the 31st of March 1979 when the last NATO and British, and indeed foreign soldier left the shores of Malta that true emancipation from the foreigner was achieved.

This date is staunchly observed as Freedom Day.

This little contest between these two parties – as to which day historically is the more important in the annals of modern Maltese history – will never be solved to the satisfaction of either party and their respective constituents, so in true compromise fashion, borrowed from the best diplomatic English traditions, both these dates, 31st March and 21st September (along with a number of others), have been enshrined as national holidays in the Malta calendar.

Neutrality in a Polarized World

As a result of, or perhaps as a rebound from its past war-experiences, modern Malta wanted to make sure that it would not be caught again in a war, world-wide or regional. It made sure of this by inserting in its Constitution the very neutrality and non-alignment of its national policies. When the Constitution was drafted and written, it must be remembered, the Cold War was in full swing and Malta was right in the middle of the East-West tussle.

Hence the Maltese Islands specifically wanted to make sure that this was fully understood by both sides: Malta was going to follow a policy of non-alignment and be equally neutral to both the East and the West.

In the modern era, especially in the aftermath of the U.S-U.S.S.R. rapprochement which, coincidentally, was sealed by the Bush-Gorbachev Summit in Malta in 1989, this professed neutrality of Malta has been seen to have paid dividends.

Malta has joined the modern nations of the modern world in a gush of modern prosperity.

Parliamentary Presidential Republic

The type of government chosen was that of a proportionately elected parliamentary representation presided over by a President. Malta,

The plaques commemorating recent important historical days: Independence, Republic and Freedom Days

finally, weaned itself from dependence on the British Crown and had its own Constitution with its own Parliament and its own laws and its own elected representatives to debate and decide its own destiny.

As Head of State, Malta no longer had the British Crown but a native-born President who would represent Malta at all the international functions and preside over many local functions. True, the President's role in its relationship to the Maltese Parliament resembled very much that of the British Monarch *vis-à-vis* the British Parliament. But Malta's President acceded to the presidency not by inheriting the throne, but by being chosen by a majority of the Members of Parliament. As is to be expected, the Presidents elected have been practically always political appointees in the sense that the political party with the majority of representatives chose someone from among its party that merited well of the party and, hopefully, of the country.

There is talk currently about modifying some aspects of the Constitution relating to this matter which will possibly see the President elected by a popular vote, somewhat on the lines of the U.S. presidential elections.

Modern Questions about Neutrality

Malta's constitution was drawn up when the super-powers, signifying the big blocks of East and West, Communism and Capitalism were at loggerheads. Malta, unwilling to be caught in the East-West super-power struggle opted for neutrality in a mostly bi-polarized world. However, since the Fall of the Berlin Wall and especially since the historic Bush-Gorbachev Summit held in Malta itself in 1989, this polarization is no longer a pressing world concern. And so many are asking whether neutrality, under the circumstances, is as important in today's world.

It may take some years for those whose generation achieved

Independence, Freedom and a Constitution – especially those surviving artificers of this three-fold bonanza for Malta – to come to terms with the changed situation in the modern world. But sensible veering to do away with unnecessary constitutional ballast and towards the adoption of progressive, forward-looking ideologies seems to be not only a political necessity but a hard-nosed condition of modern politics.

Chapter 13

The Age of Modern Communications

(Into the New Millenium)

After millenia of being a colony of some other big power in the Mediterranean Basin and/or an appendage of some world empire, the Maltese Islands have finally achieved independence and freedom and, it bears repeating, without any blood being shed. No mean feat seeing that for all these many centuries of its past history, all it had was lords and masters, rulers and sovereigns, some cruel, others brutal but definitely none benign or such as sought only this country's good. It was the turn of the native people, finally, to take the helm and guide the destinies of their own nation.

And this had to take place in the twentieth century!

And so, this tiny – by any modern international standards – archipelago-nation of Malta, Gozo, Comino and Filfla is trying to find its place in the modern world and the modern family of nations by learning from its past and churning out its own industrial and economic initiatives for self-help rather than depending on hand-outs, military or otherwise from foreign powers as it has had to do throughout its past history.

Lacking natural resources and mineral wealth, it had to fall back on other, specifically Maltese, assets and solutions.

Some examples.

Tourism

For a start, the many British Services personnel that had been assigned to Malta had liked the place so much that many of them – even after England had officially left the Islands – opted to stay on, as foreign residents on the islands. In fact, Malta has forever been an attraction for many British visitors who very often *fall in love with the place warts and all* and become repeat visitors. For many reasons: for one thing an Englishman can be undertood here. For another there are many reminders of the British presence and the British-Malta link in those reminders. And in spite of the spurts of antagonism from some Maltese in their over-patriotic excesses, the Englishman is well liked by and large by a majority of the population.

His long sojourn in Malta is viewed on the whole as having been a civilizing influence and very few Maltese (more so the many anglophiles) would have it otherwise. The many Maltese who married the British servicemen stationed in Malta have also contributed in no small measure to the good relations existing between the two nations. In fact a great number of Maltese have become British subjects and a number of Maltese are fanatic supporters of anything British, including soccer teams and Guinness.

So a flourishing industry in tourism, selling Malta as the ideal place for sea and sun and history, was initiated first to the British tourist (quite an easy sell, in a way) and later to other markets.

The concerted effort over many years has paid off and Malta is now among the more established tourist venues in Europe with visitors coming from Finland, Scandinavia, Russia, France, Spain besides all the corners of the British Isles.

And tourism has brought about in its wake another historical quirk: with the openness to all nations, oddly enough a result of the fight for democracy that the Second World War had come to symbolize, Malta began hosting visitors even from its geographically close neighbour and friend-turned-war-time-enemy, neighbouring Italy. As well as Malta's (because Britain's) eternal enemy, Germany.

Tourism – and the money it brings – can heal all wounds. It can also make strange bed-fellows. Another reason why Malta seems to be the preferred destination of many Germans who, surprised, detect no animosity from the Maltese, because there is none.

Tourism opens up all boundaries and removes limitations. Whoever can pay is made welcome. In fact, for a time, there was even a special status granted to visitors from Libya and North Africa – for gone now were, by and large, the traditional ethnic animosities felt by the Maltese against the Arab and especially against the Moslem, both long considered inimical invaders in Malta's history. Or the Turk for that matter: for a brisk trade with a direct air-link to Istanbul will brook no discrimination based on Great Siege memories.

No need to say that, as in other countries, in Malta, too, tourism has spawned, in a ripple-effect syndrome, a number of industries directly related to it which, given the limited resources in terms of area and the local natural environment has created a lot of public griping about the unbearable strain that all this expansion will bring to the Maltese Islands. There is a lot of talk about sustainable development which has a poignantly alarming sound in the Maltese islands with their very limited natural resources and space.

As a result, recently there has been a movement afoot to diversify and branch off into encouraging the up-market tourist by luring more than just the sun-sand-and-sea visitors to Malta. Malta has a lot more to offer by way of cultural and historical attractions. And so a drive for the up-market tourist has been launched so that rather than large numbers of package-deal tourists with the obvious strain this is having on the local environment, Malta will see a smaller number of substantial visitors interested in her cultural heritage and willing to spend more, with less exploitation of the environment.

Whether this is an idea whose time has come and for which Malta is ready has still to be seen. The sub-structure as well as the infra-structure has to come up to par before high-spending tourists can be attracted here.

The harbour that witnessed centuries of conflict now welcomes cruise ships and luxury liners

The new international airport at Gudja welcomes thousands of tourists

Whatever the outcome of this new drive, a country cannot survive on one source of revenue, no matter how appealing and/or popular. The on-again off-again see-saw tourist business that depends on so many factors, mostly a very healthy world economy, national well-being and political stability of the originating countries, can suffer occasional slumps. And tourism has been the victim of many such slumps. Whatever the future holds, there is no denying that tourism itself and the ancillary industries linked to tourism have created many job opportunities which in the past were not even heard of. Yet in an uncertain tourism market, one has to hedge one's bets. This can only happen by industrial diversification.

Industrial diversification

Actually Malta realized early on that it could not rely solely on tourism for its sustenance: it had to diversify. Small light industries that would limit themselves to manufacturing products, especially such as were non-polluting, such as textiles, electronics, shoes, and such like became the new vogue in the immediate post-Independence era. These were located in the industrial estates that mushroomed all over.

Since wages compared favourably with respect to Europe (in other, practical, words: labour was cheaper here) many industrialists from Germany and England and Italy were attracted to the local scene. And the small industries began to flourish. This had an impact on Malta and the Maltese not only economically but also sociologically.

Many of these factory-workers were young men and women (mostly women), who for the first time in their young lives found they could earn money from a job of their very own. This gave them self-pride. But they also thereby achieved financial emancipation from their parents and independence from their family. For whereas to date, young people stayed home as dependents on their parents till they married (to partners often ear-marked by or negotiated for them by their elders), now they began to feel masters of their own destiny, earning their own way to do with their earnings – and their lives – whatever they wanted. Even unto marrying when and whom they felt like, or, shockingly socially scandalous of all, not to marry at all but cohabit as live-ins. This was further abetted by the fact that these young people did not feel duty-bound anymore to take care of their parents in their old age: the State did that with generous social security and pension benefits to all its citizens.

The sociological impact that this new post-Independence emancipation brought about, mostly in terms of new life-styles, has still to be fully studied, for Malta has never been the same since and much talk is heard about *lost family values* which often means lack of official Church-marriages, or even – something unheard of in theocratic Catholic Malta – civil ones.

No need to say, even this happy marriage between industry and local labour in time ran into a snag: as the local standard of living improved and wages had to be continually up-graded, mostly because of a labour force ever anxious to have more in an Olivertwistian craving for a bigger piece of the pie and egged on by aggressive labour unions, most foreign companies investing in local labour began to feel the pinch.

They realized that the local labour force was not the same competitive (read: cheap) market in which they had originally invested, and so a number of companies began to close shop and move camp to emerging and cheaper labour markets. With the result that other employment opportunities had to be created for still further diversification because the Maltese labourer was now contaminated with this virus called the good life. In the world of modern technology, such other industrial outlets are being sought from among the computer-chips and communications industries.

The Shipyards

One of the more important institutions in Malta, a country known for its sea-faring people and one that goes back centuries, is its

Industrial estates have sprouted all over

The dockyard handles shipbuilding and ship repair

MALTA: A PANORAMIC HISTORY

famous shipyards. Ever since the times of the Hospitallers, a mighty naval power in its own time, but more so during the British period with its powerful navy and still more so during the war, Malta had achieved a name for itself as an important haven where ships could dock and have all the re-fitting done to them in a professional manner. Here ships, even those bombed out of their hulls during a war and barely able to limp into port, could be repaired and refitted, to go out and fight again. Granted that repairs often took place on *floating docks* before the construction of the permanent docks. But repaired they were in Malta's thriving dockyard.

So why not exploit the already functioning dockyard and expand it into ship-building besides ship-repair? As a modern yard with modern and up-to-date facilities it could attract contracts from all over the world. For this, a number of developments were planned and executed: like the construction of a dry-dock which was achieved by financial and engineering aid from Communist China under the Mintoff administration.

And while one is at it why not exploit the natural assets of the Grand Harbour to make it a haven for cruise ships by constructing modern quays, and bid to make Malta a base for some of them? Why not, in fact, establish a mercantile ship company called Sea Malta?

All this sea-faring-ness has in the modern times expanded to a very busy and hectic cruise and mercantile ship movement in the Grand Harbour which includes a tank-cleaning service at Ft Ricasoli – to empty tankers of all gases/oils before entering the dockyard for repairs as well as making Malta a home-base for Mediterranean cruise companies.

Freeports and Hub-Concepts

Not only that. The shipping activity has overflowed to the other side of the Grand Harbour, to Marsaxlokk Bay. Here the concept of developing Malta as a freeport – a shipping hub – is already under way, and expanding yearly. Under this concept, cargo ships from all over the world can off-load their containers in Malta and from here they are forwarded to their respective destinations. This procedure is a tempting proposition to many shipping companies: it saves them a lot of time and money. Malta's historic maritime destiny in the centre of the Mediterranean Sea is being channelled into peaceful and lucrative modern-day commercial ventures.

And talking about shipping: Malta has become one of the foremost nations with registered tonnage to its name carrying its flag worldwide.

The same hub-concept is being adopted for air cargo which will then put to good use the old passenger airport (which has been supplanted by the ultra-modern new one).

Land Development

Another boom that has had questionable effects on Malta is the one taking place in the property market. A more liberal approach in recent years by the governmental administration to foreign land-ownership and an opening up of the market to the liberalism of the demand-and-supply economics has brought about a sharp increase in land-prices. This has created an imbalance. When compared to mainland Europe local properties sound like a cheap and easily affordable investment, and so a European investor is ready to pay the price asked. However, such low European prices are very high by local standards (since wages are also lower than the European average) and hence there is an impasse. This problem has to be addressed – though it may never be solved since the availability of this commodity called land is limited by the very narrow confines and area of these small islands and there is only so much property to go around. This makes it all the more valuable, and at the same time sought after.

The modern development trends of business-plazas,

supermarkets and holiday-complexes make huge demands on land, a commodity of which Malta does not have a great abundance. The result is that agricultural land is being built up, the country-side (what little there is to start with) devastated, already teeming cities are made denser and once peaceful hamlets over-developed.

The price of progress, say some. Environmental suicide, assert others. Malta has truly joined the modern era on all fronts.

Banking and other things

Malta has joined the world as well on the banking front with a more liberalized banking system than it had ever enjoyed to date, away from the tight-fisted money policies which saw both local Maltese residents (clandestinely) and foreign ones (legally) investing their moneys abroad. The present-day liberal banking policy opened up new markets and new horizons. Now there is an influx of all sorts of moneys, and of all colour and of all nations being invested here.

Added to all this economic boom is the effort of the government to make Malta share in the off-shore banking bonanza which by all reports seems to be flourishing and doing well indeed. The success that Malta has had in this field will perhaps help one to begin to understand the Malta Success Story in Banking – with more promised as tiny Malta enlarges the activities being transacted in its fledgling Stock Market. This success story seems to be repeated on all financial fronts – making of Malta a solid economic success story all over. The fact that it is such a stable country politically speaking must also help inspire confidence in investors.

In fact the political climate is so stable in Malta at the time that not only are many foreigners investing their goods and wealth in Malta, but an ever-increasing number of foreigners are opting to find ways and means to settle and work in Malta. Some do it in their yachts – in the recently set-up yacht marinas. Others are doing it as foreign residents who opt to settle in this country. Other foreigners still, such as those whose business or jobs take them to the oil-rich

Yacht marinas – like the one at Msida – cater for a different kind of tourist

countries, have discovered that they can adopt Malta as a base where they can safely leave their family as they go on their month-on-month-off stints. Malta looks as good a base as any for the education of foreign children in terms of international schools, open schools, European schools and even local English-medium schools. The foreigners find themselves in a friendly environment – with the thousands of years of dealing with foreigners, the Maltese have become past masters in the art and hence foreigners find themselves at home here.

However, it is not merely the economic indicators that measure a country's affluence. Material wealth and well-being avails a country very little until and unless such affluence overflows into and benefits the cultural, educational and human development fields. And that is precisely what has happened in Malta. In recent years we have seen a bursting forth, indeed a flourishing of the arts, with such areas as drama, music, painting, sculpture, writing taking centre stage. Malta's own sons and daughters, who till yesterday were deemed incapable of running their own country, are now shining forth not only locally but on the international scene. Mention must be made of the many Maltese names that have carried the honour of their country abroad in the world of classical music. Others in other fields have merited equally well and here it is enough to note the explosion in the writing world where authoritative books researched by Maltese and published in Malta have literally inundated the market.

This varied menu of cultural productivity must surely be considered as a fair indicator of the (healthy) state of the arts in the country, which in turn will serve as a very encouraging environment for the budding talented youngsters.

One could go on – especially if one were to isolate the island of Gozo as a separate success story and sing its praises for having gone modern and yet retained its particular quaintness and attraction in a world making heavy demands on its sub-structure.

Surely there must be some fly in the ointment as compounded by the Maltese Islands? Oh yes!

The Church-State relationship

One word must be said about the peculiar relationship of the Church and the State in Malta.

There is a rock-solid tradition and belief, based on the narration found in the biblical book of the Acts of the Apostles, that St Paul visited the Maltese Islands and converted the natives to Christianity. (The chapter on St Paul's shipwreck in Malta goes into all the details).

So ever since the year 60 A.D. Malta has been uninterruptedly Christian and her Christianity has forever been of the apostolic and Roman kind. Uninterruptedly, that is, barring the hiatus of Arab Rule when according to some historians, in keeping with the prevalent customs of the time, a conquering nation imposed its creed and its form of government on the conquered.

Under the Hospitallers, as we have seen, who were Christian to the core and with whose defence of the faith against the infidel Malta's destiny was solidly linked – for economic reasons besides religious ones – the Catholic-Christian faith was still further entrenched in these islands. In fact, with the terrifying aid of the formidable Inquisition (even though in its milder, Roman form here), the Catholic Faith was well and truly established in Malta. As to the British, these happened to be Christian, though of the Anglican not the Roman Catholic persuasion and in their policy of not openly opposing or upsetting the local *status quo*, did not overtly try to suppress the Catholicism of Malta – though they did it by other more subtle means such as favouring or promoting Maltese who converted to Protestantism or were Protestants.

The Roman Catholic Faith, therefore, has been considered in the common thinking of the majority of the people of Malta as its bulwark against all infidel (and not so infidel, such as Protestant-

Christian) attacks to the integrity of the islands. It has also been considered as the measure of God's predilection for his people – sealed by miracles performed especially when under dire stress (the Great Siege of 1565, and the Second World War to cite two major ones) when Malta was at the end of its tether and ready to surrender, only to be sensationally saved by the intervention from on high.

There is no doubting the fact that, as we have seen, the kind of repressive measures and extreme deterrents used by the Inquisition in Malta, even though the one in Malta was the milder Roman kind, helped to keep the believing people in line, and the rest – whatever few non-Catholics there might have been on the islands – in fear of doing anything wrong. This, abetted with the periodic teaching of the supremacy of the spiritual authority that even transcended into and governed the purely secular or even political spheres, gave the Church as an institution in Malta a lot of power.

Besides, in a general environment where the clerics were usually the more educated members of the community and where the faithful turned to them for the resolution of all sorts of problems, spiritual, personal, economical and otherwise, it was inevitable that the clergy should have a great amount of power in this sort of society.

As a result, not only was the Church as an institution the supreme authority in these islands, but since the Church in concrete terms, meant the Bishops and the clergy, and the monks and the friars and the nuns – these ended up being the *confidence-persons* of the nation.

It is in this context of supreme power that the slapping of an interdict by the Church Hierarchy has to be seen – whether in the 30's in the time of Strickland – or in the 60's in the time of Mintoff's heyday as the Labour Party's unquestioned leader.

In the 60's – to reduce to its basic elements a confrontation that was long in coming – the Church headed by Archbishop Michael Gonzi did not like the way the Malta Labour Party was veering. The Archbishop, who himself had at one time been a member of parliament elected from the ranks of the Labour Party, knew a thing or two about politics. But in the 60's, for various reasons (among which was Mintoff's proposal to integrate Malta with Britain which would have made all of Protestant England's laws automatically the laws of Catholic Malta and thus could have been seen as an effort to undermine the Church's hold on the faithful Catholics), Archbishop Gonzi decreed that any Maltese citizen who voted for the Labour Party committed a mortal sin and was also slapped with an interdict. This meant that a Maltese Catholic was unable to receive the sacraments, i.e., be baptized, attend Mass, receive communion, be married in Church, or receive Catholic burial or be buried in hallowed ground.

In other words, a faithful Maltese Catholic who wanted to follow the Church's teaching could not, in conscience, vote Labour. Or else he was ostracized.

This Church edict may have been the result of a miscalculation or bad advice; for no one could have foreseen that thousands of Labour Party supporters – which at this time had already won over the sympathies of Malta's strongest union, the General Workers' Union – would go ahead and vote Labour in defiance of Church ban. But thousands did.

And ever since then, Malta has witnessed the tragedy of the rift between the Labour Party and the Catholic Church which has widened ever more and more. Many practising Catholics unwilling to give up their Labourite sympathies left the Church. Many families whose political loyalties split them apart witnessed a further split in Church affiliation. And many Labourites – abetted by workers from the 'Yards and other such institutions where the Labour-G.W.U tandem was strongest – simply turned violent against a Church that was seen to be oppressing the poor (many of Labour's supporters came from the ordinary labour force) and favouring the rich (represented by the clergy that mostly abetted the other party, the Nationalists).

These are, naturally, merely fleeting highlights of a struggle that went on for many decades; that, in fact, is still going on. In the end, it resulted in an out-and-out effort on the part of the Labour Party to wean Malta and the political field from the influence of the Church.

The many laws that the Labour Party enacted when in power are seen precisely as indicators aiming in that direction. The Marriage Act of 1975 was just one such effort: it broke new ground, doing the unthinkable in Malta where all marriages had hitherto been Church marriages, and even a non-Catholic, or worse, a non-believer marrying a Maltese was obliged to marry *in Church* promising to bring up the children as Catholics. This marriage-law reform allowed for the first time the possibility of civil marriage. Such a ploy, besides providing a way out for those *interdicted* or *excommunicated* Maltese Catholics (who, forbidden a Church wedding were now able to have their union recognized by the State, civilly), also opened the way up for the *laicization* of Malta. Henceforth, civil marriage was another option to anybody who so wanted to marry and it was equally valid and so recognized by the State of Malta for all practical purposes of legitimacy of off-spring and disposition of marital assets.

Another thorn in the side of the Labour Party was the influence of the Church through its well-administered and tightly controlled educational institutions. A way had to be found to break this Church monopoly and especially this systematic grinding of what Labour saw as Church yes-men among the elite upper-class to the detriment of the lower, labour echelons.

So when in power and in government, the Labour Party forced the Church in Malta to open up its school doors to all children who wanted to attend without any discrimination, or special treatment for those Catholics in good standing versus those who were not; or for those who could pay as against those who could not afford (the high Church fees). After all, Labour insisted, Christ opted for the poor and so should the Church.

This education tussle became a sore issue and rather than cave in and open its doors indiscriminately to all, the Catholic Church preferred to close its schools to sort out the mess if nothing else.

Another piece of legislation enacted by the Labour Party when in government which was seen as a direct hit against the Church related to the matter of Church-land for re-distribution. The accusation was made that the Church was the biggest land-owner in Malta and this was against the spirit of poverty preached by Christ in the gospel: as were the excessive festivities associated with the celebration of the village festas.

To remedy the first, a number of Church properties were appropriated by the Labour government to be distributed. And to remedy the second, the traditional village festas were allowed to be celebrated only on Sundays and not on the day the feast fell, and then without any of the powerful petards or bomb-blasts and shorn of frenzied paraphernalia.

One may consider all this as picayunish nit-picking. But in the context of what happened in the 60's and 70's in Catholic Malta, this was radical indeed. And whether one likes it or not, the radical changes that the Labour Party introduced into Malta were part of a purposeful plan: to undermine the power of the Catholic Church. In the process it turned out to be a weaning experience: the populace began to believe it could stand on its own two feet and think with its own mind even in defiance of authority. This was something unheard of in Malta till then – with a submissive populace always ready to do the will of the superior power, whether colonial, political or ecclesiastical.

Much of this, one must remember, happened in Malta before that epoch-making Church gathering in Rome called the Second Vatican Council – even though the Church-State struggle went on through the 70's, the spirit of Vatican II had not penetrated into the mass-mentality. (Some say it is barely visible now, in the 90's in Malta – which has retained its traditional old Catholic conservative ways of thinking and acting as far as religion is concerned.)

The Village Festa remains a heavy dose of folklore and faith

The Good Friday procession draws big crowds and participants. *Above:* Banners with "The Seven Words"; *left:* the Penitentes with shackled feet; *below:* the "Redeemer", one of the statues carried shoulder-high

In retrospect, there are those who question whether the Labour Party tried to hurry the pace too much by trying to impose sociological as well as economic structures, and especially secular, lay ones on a Catholic country that may not have been ready for them. And as often happens with things that come before their time, they are considered radical, upsetting or unwelcome.

One such other diplomatic ploy which took place under the Labour administration and which was seen as an effort to undercut the Catholic Church's hold on Catholic Malta was the concept of *pluralism in divine worship* whereby other religious beliefs besides the Catholic faith were allowed to establish a Church, temple, synagogue or mosque. To date the only non-Catholic houses of worship that had been allowed were the Protestant, mostly Anglican, Churches introduced here during the British Colonial period. Even then these were mostly meant for the convenience and use of British Administrative and Services Personnel on the islands.

However, the modifications introduced in the 60's and 70's allowed all religions – not only the mainstream Christian faiths but literally all religions – the facility to establish a base in Malta. Thus, in short order, a mosque was built, with financing from Libya mostly, for the convenince of the Moslem faithful on the island. And the evangelical Christian groups along with the Baptists and Jehovah's Witnesses soon set up a place of worship here as well. As did the Bahai's and the Unification Church and the Latter Day Saints (Mormons) as indeed a number of others. All this opened up Malta and the Maltese to other faiths in their own home grounds – which to date they had only read about or visited when abroad.

In all this, there were those – especially among the old-style Catholics – who looked on the intrusion of these foreign faiths as a further loss of the exclusive hold that the Catholic Faith should have on the Catholic Maltese. The Constitution of Malta, they clamoured, still holds the Roman Catholic Faith as the only faith of the Maltese islands. That was back in the 70's.

Today, the idea of pluralism and religious tolerance which not merely tolerates but accepts other religions 'as other' is gaining ground in modern Malta. In fact, it must be admitted that much of what the Labour Party tried to do prematurely is being done today by the sheer force of the media explosion in the field of modern communications. As was to be expected, Malta could no longer remain an isolated out-post in the world of today and things that the rest of the world suffers through, good and bad, also take place in Malta: the drug-problem; the AIDS epidemic; the free-love age-groups; the live-ins; single parent families; unwed mothers; open relationships of the homosexual kind.

All these have come to Malta's shores in spite of the over-protectiveness in which the local population has been wrapped. And more is bound to come – as Malta becomes ever more and more secular and more and more pluralistic. So why not pluralism in religious faiths and religious practices?

All of which makes the nostalgic yearn for the good old days when good was good and bad was bad and the Church had absolute control over the morality of the nation. Only time will tell who is right and whether Malta as an independent nation has been served well by her politicians and her Church leaders.

This holds especially true for the Labour Party which has come a long way from the time when luminaries like Dr (later Sir) Paul Boffa guided its destinies – and Malta's. ·

Europe-bound?

In this particular mine-field called Malta's bid to join the European Union, there are various and very blatantly opposite opinions (basically two, and diametrically opposed). The Malta Labour Party and its sympathizers paint a dreary, frightening and dire picture of the consequences of Malta's joining the European Union and definitely oppose such a move in favour of joining an E.F.T.A-type (European Free Trade) association. The Nationalist Party and its supporters want full membership with the European Union with

Malta as one of the member-states and see nothing but rosy paths ahead as a result of Malta's membership.

Listening to the arguments from either side, one gets the impression that two completely different worlds have met in one little group of small islands.

The Labour Party although opposed to Malta's entry into the European Union, favours E.F.T.A. because, so the argument goes, for a small country like Malta, joining Europe will mean playing second fiddle to the big nations like Germany, France and England. The European Union itself is already running on two tracks: the advanced nations and the less advanced within the Union. Malta, coming late on the scene, will have a harder time of it and will never catch up with the less advanced, still less with the more advanced members. Thus the hard-earned emancipation from the foreigner that Malta has attained will be to no avail in a Union in which Malta finds itself in a league of second-class, or even third class nations. More drastically still will Malta's hard-won independence be lost if the Maltese will have to measure up to all the various bureaucratic injunctions about all sorts of economic, agricultural and even environmental legislation issuing from Brussels. Other arguments brought forward against joining are the less serious warning of a greater AIDS proliferation from contact with Europe and such things.

The General Workers' Union – one of the most powerful unions in Malta – although having technically and officially severed its once very strong tandem with the Labour Party and therefore supposedly coming to independent conclusions, abets the Labour Party's stand that Europe is bad for Malta.

Irrespective of anything else, this Europe-or-bust policy forced the Nationalist Party, so claims the Labour Party, to precipitately pass many measures that are proving detrimental to Malta's own well-being. Malta is strapped with quickie legislation hurried through without proper discussion and enough mulling over.

One such blatant example – according to the Labour Party – was the introduction of V.A.T.: the Value Added Tax, which meant a re-structuring of the tax-system of Malta, a re-structuring that resulted in a lot of hardship to small businesses. That it also meant a ferreting out of the countless number of small entrepreneurs that never declared their true and total income to the Taxman, and that therefore did not give a true picture of the economic situation of the islands, is diplomatically hushed over.

Another thorn in the side of the Labour Party in what is perceived as the Nationalists' headlong drive to join the European Club is the influence that this European Union will have on Malta's national heritage, its culture and language. For on the one hand, there is no doubt that the Labour Party, with its roots deep in the heart of the humbler echelons of Maltese society, has if anything, proclaimed itself as the defender of the down-and-outer, the down-trodden, the ordinary Maltese labourer – as its name suggests.

The Nationalists, on the other hand, were at one time in their past strong Italian sympathizers, spoke only Italian and even had their newspaper in that language and abetted Malta's amalgamation with the Italian peninsula.

With such a not-overly patriotic background of the Nationalist Party, some Labourites fear that the future of the Maltese language, Maltese culture, and Maltese education is very much in doubt as and when Malta joins Europe. It stands to be engulfed by the big powers as it had not been in the wars it so gallantly fought in the past to preserve its Maltese and Catholic identity.

Another concession that the Malta Labour Party considers a surrender to European pressure on the part of the Nationalist Party is the opening up of the Maltese land market to foreign speculators – especially when there is such a limited amount of local resources in land-surface area to go around. But then again, if Malta is to join Europe and be an equal partner with the big boys, it has to act fast with an open-market policy with all that this entails in all its aspects including opening its doors to foreign investment as well – wherever it comes from.

There is no doubt that there can be many reservations about Malta's joining the European Union. Some verge on the national level interest, others on the scary tactics level, and they have to be worked out by a consensus of the majority of the population with a national referendum.

There is no question that by joining the European Union, Malta stands to lose some of its identity. The status and future of the Maltese language is one such matter which cannot be lightly dismissed for there is a very strong patriotic movement in Malta which contends that its language is part of its identity. However, in a world gone universal, it is difficult today to figure out any pocket anywhere preserving itself in a cocoon of isolation especially since Malta is lucky enough to have been associated with that universal language, English.

Another more serious consideration centres around the status of the Catholic faith. In this regard the Nationalist Party did its best, bending over backwards by diplomatic and other means to help the Church retain its place of honour. In fact, in the Church-State agreement in which Church property was *purchased* by the State, the terms worked out were most advantageous to the Church. And more recently, the (revised) Marriage Act conceded, among other things, to Church tribunals the power to have Church annulments recognized as civil annulments as well.

October 1996

The above political considerations which at the time of writing sounded so academic received a very realistic focus in the autumn of 1996. The Nationalist Party in government with its leader, Dr Eddie Fenech Adami, as Malta's premier felt that the time was ripe to call fresh elections. The P.N. was, after all, close to the end of its second five-year mandate and it felt that it was practically a shoe-in for a third term.

However, by an overwhelming majority of votes, the Maltese electorate voted the Malta Labour Party led by Dr Alfred Sant into power. One of the first acts of the new Labour government – as promised in the electoral manifesto – was to withdraw Malta's participation in the Partnership for Peace (PfP). The Nationalists had joined this partnership against the Labourite objections that this ran counter to Malta's constitutional neutrality.

The other electoral promise that received immediate action on Labour's accession to power was to 'freeze' Malta's application to join the European Union, an application that had been pending for some time anyhow.

Another Labour electoral manifesto promise was to abolish VAT. Even though VAT had come to be associated with Malta's bid to join Europe and thus submit to European fiscal policies, still realistically speaking few governments can survive or function without the revenue from tax-collection by whatever name it is called.

To the credit of Malta it must be said that the change in administration from the Nationalist Party to the Labour Party took place in the most democratic of ways and the smoothest of handovers. The electoral campaign itself, though hard-fought, was not dirty or, worse, bloody, but most civilized as befits a nation that is politically mature.

As is to be expected in politics, the new Labour government, to earn its stripes, has been clamouring, in its first few months in office, about the financial 'mess' it has found. And true to script, the P.N., now on the other side of the bench in opposition, keeps harping on the lack of direction of the present Labour administration with its errant fiscal and other policies.

There is no doubt that the Malta Labour Party under its leader, Harvard-educated Dr Alfred Sant, has to prove its mettle. The electoral campaign saw an up-and-coming politician in the person of Alfred Sant who came practically out of nowhere to rise out of the Labour ranks and galvanize his party into a stunning upset victory.

September 1998

Although, as stated above, the Labour government had a majority of the popular vote, it only had a one seat majority in parliament. In September 1998, Dr Sant called fresh elections when a Labour member of parliament voted against the party policies.

The Nationalist Party was returned to government with Dr Eddie Fenech Adami again becoming Prime Minister. Malta's application to join the European Union was re-activated and VAT re-introduced.

In the foregoing, the impression might have been given that Malta's political arena is a two-party system: the Malta Labour Party and the Nationalist Party. To round off the picture and to give as objective a view of the situation as possible, it must also be said that recently in Malta a group of people with young ideals has joined the fray as a political party. They call themselves 'Alternattiva Demokratika' (Democratic Alternative) and hope to be a wedge between what they see as vested interests on the part of both the major power-wielding and power-brokering parties in Malta: the Labour Party and the Nationalist Party, viewed both as working in tandem and for each other's mutual benefit in spite of the apparent show of disagreement in public. The fact that the founders were two young members of the Malta Labour Party, Dr Wenzu Mintoff and Dr Toni Abela, who for ideological as well as moral reasons seceded from that Party added weight to their stands. *Alternattiva Demokratika* has become a pressure group that talks out about many controversial issues other parties prefer not to broach.

However, in the October 1996 and September 1998 elections, AD did not fare so well. In fact it lost ground over the previous elections and hence it also lost much of its clout.

Tailpiece

As one looks – panoramically – at the history of these Maltese Islands, one big factor should have stood out in it all. The people of these islands have for the many thousands of years of their history been ruled by others. They have never been masters of their own destiny. The early settlers, the Neolithic inhabitants, who left us their majestic temples, left us little to go by as to their identity and their role on the islands. But starting with the Phoenicians and the Carthaginians, the local Maltese were ruled by others. In fact, the first really local settlers may have been the Phoenicians and the Carthaginians. Under the Romans, Malta was part of the Roman Empire and as such was ruled by a Praetor or a representative of the Roman Emperors who ruled as governor. The same can be said when Malta formed part of the Byzantine Empire.

Under the Moslem-Arabs it is very doubtful whether the Maltese were even allowed to stay in their native land still less govern and rule. Under the Normans, Malta was a fiefdom. As it was under the Anjevins and the Aragonese.

Under the aristocratic Hospitallers, who ruled like monarchs over this republic, the only place in this structured society for the local Maltese was as enforced labourers – as oarsmen, builders, servants, donats, and such like. These celibate gentlemen even managed to spurn the semblance of local government in the shape of the local governing body: the *università dei grani*, limited as its ambit of power and administration happened to be.

Things were no different under Colonial Rule – whether French or British: the Maltese could not advance anywhere beyond certain lower clerical echelons. In fact, they were kept positively out of matters dealing with the destiny and government of their own country.

It is not surprising that with these many thousands of years as a subservient nation – to outsiders on its own soil – Malta should feel proud that at last, in this twentieth century, it has achieved not only independence but a respectable position in the family of nations.

The story in post-Independence Malta has been very different. Gone is the time when the answer to the endemic poverty of the islanders was to ship its people in mass emigration in cattle boats to Australia, Canada and anywhere else that would accept them. Now not only is there employment for almost everybody, not only is there a good and indeed high standard of living, not only are most of the casualties of society catered to by a safety-net in a caring social system that does not allow degeneration into homelessness or vagrant wandering but, the highest accolade of all, even the Maltese migrants – those who once emigrated to foreign lands to stave off poverty and starvation – are realizing that they would be better off back home. Call it nostalgia, call it practicality. But partly it also stems from the solid belief in Malta's present course of action that places it among the more advanced in the developing nations, and bodes well for confidence in her future. Malta is experiencing what is known as reverse-migration: the ex-patriots are coming back to re-settle, in their homeland, in Malta as well as Gozo.

And as one goes around, the tell-tale house-names say it all: *God bless America*, says one complete with the American eagle. *Stars and Stripes forever*, says another. *Mapleleaf House*. *Kangaroo House* – dead give-aways as to where these returned migrants are coming from.

All this would not have happened if Malta were still that place to run away from or that one would want to leave at the first opportunity. As it was once with the lack of employment opportunities and lack of a decent standard of living. By and large, it must be admitted that at present Malta has a high standard of living, comparable with anywhere in the developed world, without too many of the pitfalls and the disadvantages prevalent in these big countries. And so, Malta has become a much sought-after place in which to settle down.

However, reverse-migrants might be accused of nostalgic ties to the homeland, ties which were never severed. A more objective – though perhaps less welcome – yardstick of Malta's present affluent status is the presence of the alarming number of illegal immigrants. Not only those hailing from the North African countries, most of whom are ready to enter into arranged civil marriage with the locals to attain *ipso facto* immediate Maltese citizenship, but even from the ex-East European nations – refugees from ex-Yugoslavia, exiles from Russia and other places. The local papers are also full of repatriation-cases of other people from other, supposedly affluent, European nations as well.

For a number of other people from the developed countries are seeking Malta: land speculators from the rest of Europe, industrialists from Germany, and – the best tribute of all – the old Colonializers, the British, themselves who come for the sea and the sun and, often, even for a job in this politically stable, economically affluent mecca of the Mediterranean.

For Malta at present seems to be enjoying an unprecedented standard of living socially, politically, economically in a free market economy which only the blind can miss. Sure there are many things that need to be done; many reforms to be undertaken; many projects that need completion.

But then that is the way it should be: otherwise what would we have all those parliamentarians for? And all those commissions? And all those municipal councils?

And all those – more than a quarter of a million citizens – who imagine themselves to be arm-chair prime ministers, and want to run the country *their* way?

Sources

Agius, A. J. *The Genesis of Freemasonry in Malta (1730-1843)*. Valletta, Malta, 1993 (published by the author).

Agius, Emmanuel. *Social Consciousness of the Church in Malta, 1891-1921*. Malta: Media Centre Publ., 1991.

Air Battle of Malta, The. The official Account of the R.A.F. in Malta, June 1940-Nov 1942. London: H.M.Stationery Office, 1944.

Attard, Joseph. *The Knights of Malta*. Malta: Publishers Enterprises Group (PEG) Ltd, 1992.

____, *Britain and Malta, the Story of an Era*. Malta: Publishers Enterprises Group (PEG) Ltd,1988.

Attard, Lawrence,Rev. *Early Maltese emigration: 1900-1914*. Malta: Gulf Publ., 1983

____, *The Great Exodus: 1914-39*. Malta: Publishers Enterprises Group (PEG) Ltd, 1989.

Azzopardi, John, Rev. *Mdina and the Earthquake of 1693*. Malta: Heritage Books, undated.

Bladger, George Percy. *Description of Malta and Gozo*. Malta: Valletta Publ Co., 1989.

Blouet, Brian. *The Story of Malta*. Malta: Progress Press, 1993.

Bonanno, Anthony. *Malta, an archaeological paradise*. Malta: M.J. Press, 1995.

Bonnici, Alexander, O.F.M. Conv. *Storja tal-Inkiżizzjoni ta' Malta*. (3 vols). Malta: Reliġjon u Ħajja.

____, *Malta Kattolika fil-Ħajja Mqallba tas-Seklu XX*.

____, *Familji Mfarrkin f'Malta ta' l-Imgħoddi*.

Borg, C.L.*Salute to Maltese Infantrymen*. Valletta Publ. Co.,1990.

Bradford, Ernle.*The Siege: Malta 1940-43*. Penguin Books, 1987.

____, *The Great Siege, Malta 1565*. Penguin Books, 1964.

Elliott, Peter. *A Naval History of Malta: 1789-1979*. London: Grafton Books, 1989.

Ellul, Joseph. *1565, the Great Siege of Malta*. Malta: published by the author, 1992.

Ellul, Joseph S. *Malta's Pre-diluvian Culture*. Malta: published by the author, 1989.

Ellul Mercer, Guzè. *Taħt in-Nar*. Malta: Klabb Kotba Maltin,1986.

Fiorini, Stanley *and* Mallia Milanes, Victor (ed). *Malta, A Case Study in International Cross-Currents*. Malta: Univ. Press, 1991.

Fiorini, Stanley. *Santo Spirito Hospital at Rabat, Malta*. Malta: DOI, 1987.

Frendo, Henry. *The Epic of Malta. The Pictorial Survey*. Valletta Publ. Co, 1990.

____, *Malta's Quest for Independence*. Malta: Valletta Publ. Co, 1994.

Galea, M. *The Palace of the Grand Masters and the Armoury*. Malta: M.J. Publ, 1990.

____, *Malta Diary of a War*. Malta: Publishers Enterprises Group (PEG) Ltd, 1990

Ganado, Herbert. *Rajt Malta Tinbidel*. (4 vols). Malta: Interprint, 1977.

Gaullaumier, Alfred. Bliet u Rħula ta' Malta. Malta: Valletta Publ. Co., 1987.

Gerada-Azzopardi, Eric *and* Zuber, Christian. *Malta, an Island Republic*. Dalroisse Publications, undated.

Ġrajjet Malta: Education Department text-book based on Prof Andrew Vella's 'Storja ta' Malta'. Malta: Interprint, 1983.

Kilin. *A Maltese Mosaic*. Malta: published by the author, 1990.

Mallia Milanes, Victor *and* Scerri, Louis. *Uneasy Partnership: 1530 - 1565*. Malta: Midsea Books, 1985.

Melita Historica: quarterly published by The Malta Historical Society containing valuable research and information.

Micallef, Denise. *Malta Mitt Sena ilu*. Malta: Publishers Enterprises Group (PEG) Ltd, 1986.

Mizzi, Laurence. *Maltin fil-Gwerra*. Malta: Publishers Enterprises Group (PEG) Ltd, 1992

Pace, Anthony (ed.), *Maltese Prehistoric Art: 5000 B.C.-2500 B.C.* Malta: Progress Press, 1996.

Sire, H.J.A. *The Knights of Malta*. Yale Univ. Press, 1994.

Spiteri, Charles B. *Tifkiriet ta' l-Imghoddi*. Malta: Stamperija Indipendenza, 1993.

Treasures of Malta, a magazine published by Fondazzjoni Patrimonju Malti and N.T.O.M.

Wettinger, Godfrey. 'Malta under the Arabs' (Sunday Times 18/2/90), Allied Publications, Valletta.

____, 'Christians in Muslim Malta' (Sunday Times 8/4/90). Allied Publications, Valletta.

Zammit, Sir Themistocles. *Prehistoric Temples of Malta and Gozo*. Mayrhofer edition, 1995.

Zammit, Vincent. *Gran Mastri: Ġabra ta' Tagħrif.* Vol. I (1530-1680). Malta: Valletta Publ. Co., 1992.

Name Index